Systematic Review and Meta-Analysis

Systematic Review and Meta-Analysis
Stepwise Approach for Medical and Biomedical Researchers

Edited by

Mahsa Ghajarzadeh

*Johns Hopkins University School of Medicine,
Baltimore, MD, United States*

Nima Rezaei

Tehran University of Medical Sciences, Tehran, Iran

Sara Hanaei

*Department of Neurosurgery, Imam Khomeini Hospital Complex
(IKHC), Tehran University of Medical Sciences (TUMS), Tehran, Iran*

*Borderless Research, Advancement and Innovation in Neuroscience
Network (BRAINet), Tehran, Iran*

ELSEVIER

ACADEMIC PRESS
An imprint of Elsevier

Academic Press is an imprint of Elsevier
125 London Wall, London EC2Y 5AS, United Kingdom
525 B Street, Suite 1650, San Diego, CA 92101, United States
50 Hampshire Street, 5th Floor, Cambridge, MA 02139, United States

Notices

Knowledge and best practice in this field are constantly changing. As new research and experience broaden our understanding, changes in research methods, professional practices, or medical treatment may become necessary.

Practitioners and researchers must always rely on their own experience and knowledge in evaluating and using any information, methods, compounds, or experiments described herein. In using such information or methods they should be mindful of their own safety and the safety of others, including parties for whom they have a professional responsibility.

To the fullest extent of the law, neither the Publisher nor the authors, contributors, or editors, assume any liability for any injury and/or damage to persons or property as a matter of products liability, negligence or otherwise, or from any use or operation of any methods, products, instructions, or ideas contained in the material herein.

ISBN: 978-0-443-13428-9

For information on all Academic Press publications visit our website at
https://www.elsevier.com/books-and-journals

Publisher: Stacy Masucci
Acquisitions Editor: Chris Katsaropoulos
Editorial Project Manager: Deepak Vohra
Production Project Manager: Sharmila Kirouchenadassou
Cover Designer: Christian Bilbow

Typeset by TNQ Technologies

Working together
to grow libraries in
developing countries

www.elsevier.com • www.bookaid.org

To my lovely daughter,
Mehrsa
and my supportive husband and brother:
Mehdi & Mahyar

Contents

CHAPTER 7   Data extraction 61
Narges Ebrahimi

CHAPTER 8   Assessment of risk of bias in included studies........67
Narges Ebrahimi

CHAPTER 17   **Scientific writing in a systematic review and Meta-Analyses** **195**

Paria Dehesh

Contributors

Kiarash Aramesh
Department of Biology, Earth, and Environmental Sciences (BEES), The James F. Drane Bioethics Institute, PA, United States

Paria Dehesh
Kerman University of Medical Science, Department of Biostatistic and Epidemiology, Kerman, Iran

Narges Ebrahimi
Department of Immunology, Faculty of Medicine, Isfahan University of Medical Sciences, Isfahan, Iran; Immunodeficiency Diseases Research Center, Isfahan University of Medical Sciences, Isfahan, Iran; Isfahan Neurosciences Research Center, Isfahan University of Medical Sciences, Isfahan, Iran

Kathryn C. Fitzgerald
Department of Neurology, Johns Hopkins University School of Medicine, Baltimore, MD, United States

Mahsa Ghajarzadeh
Department of Neurology, Johns Hopkins University School of Medicine, Baltimore, MD, United States

Mehdi Mokhtari
Department of Epidemiology, Khoy University of Medical Science, Khoy, Iran

Mohsen Rastkar
Tehran University of Medical Sciences, Tehran, Iran

Masoumeh Sadeghi
Department of Epidemiology, School of Health, Mashhad University of Medical Sciences, Mashhad, Iran

Margaret Vieira
Department of Neurology, Johns Hopkins University School of Medicine, Baltimore, MD, United States

Preface

Welcome to *Systematic Review and Meta-Analysis: Stepwise Approach for Medical and Biomedical Researchers!*

These days, the need for systematic reviews and meta-analysis has been growing rapidly, and different groups need to know the gap of knowledge and the best clinical practice, etc. There are a variety of books in this field that researchers and healthcare providers have read. Still, they lack a stepwise approach for doing a systematic search, data extraction, risk of bias assessment, meta-analysis, and scientific writing of the manuscript. We tried to make the content of this book very easy to read and go through all the steps of the book with examples and practical examples.

In this book, we will learn how to:

1. Develop structured questions for systematic reviews,
2. Develop a search strategy and conduct a systematic search,
3. Extract data from included studies,
4. Do the quality assessment of included studies with different tools,
5. Perform meta-analysis in different software,
6. Interpret the results and forest plots,
7. Evaluate publication bias and heterogeneity between study results,
8. Do network meta-analysis,
9. Do a quality assessment of systematic reviews,
10. Scientific writing of systematic reviews,
11. Ethical considerations in systematic reviews.

We hope this book helps researchers conduct systematic reviews sensibly, and we look forward to hearing from you about the experiences and skills that you earned by reading this book.

Medical research: Steps toward scientific advancement

1

Mahsa Ghajarzadeh and Margaret Vieira

Department of Neurology, Johns Hopkins University School of Medicine, Baltimore, MD,
United States

Working as a healthcare provider (at any level) allows learning about new therapies, new devices, risk factors for developing certain diseases or conditions, preventive methods, prognostic factors, and survival profiles (1).

Personnel involved in healthcare, such as physicians, policy-makers, and governments, need to be knowledgeable and up-to-date on scientific topics to apply the best available evidence.

Medical research is the backbone of healthcare advancement and helps find answers to a wide range of questions and endorse future crucial research to fill knowledge gaps. Today's high-quality care results from researchers' past efforts to understand signs and symptoms, diagnostic approaches, screening methods, and therapies of certain diseases, as well as introducing novel medical devices and rehabilitation strategies. Medical research also provides a better understanding of different conditions and diseases' molecular pathways and genetic bases (2).

On the other hand, policy-makers and governments need to know the prevalence and incidence of the different medical illnesses in their society to make better strategies, plans, and budget allocation. They also need to know potential risk factors, preventive strategies, and the burden of certain diseases to modify possible leading causes of diseases and conditions to decrease health-related burdens in societies.

In general, research means an investigation that aims to contribute to knowledge development and find responses to specific questions (3).

Medical research shows its primary goals as medical care to reach conclusions regarding developing new treatments, finding new prevention methods, identifying potential risk factors, potential prognostic factors, features affecting survival, and finally, improving health-related quality of life.

Due to the data collection period, medical research can be categorized into two main groups: prospective or retrospective, and based on the study design, it can be categorized into observational or experimental (4).

In observational studies, researchers only observe conditions and phenomena and gather data without any interventions, while in interventional studies, the researchers expose subjects to a specific intervention or treatment (1).

Systematic Review and Meta-Analysis. https://doi.org/10.1016/B978-0-443-13428-9.00001-X

You can choose the study design based on time, study goals, budget, and personnel.

The first step for any study is determining a specific study question, and then defining the best study type to answer your research question. Afterward, you may gather information, analyze data, interpret the results, and report the results. Application of the results by physicians to specific groups of patients needs precision and knowledge.

Over the past years, there has been a force toward evidence-based medicine practice, integrating the best research findings, clinical expertise, and individual patient circumstances (5). It provides the opportunity to apply high-quality clinical research in decision-making for individual patients (5).

One of the advantages of evidence-based practice is the development of systematic reviews and meta-analyses, methods by which researchers summarize the results of previously published studies after a sensitive search, critical appraisal, and proper pooling methods.

The evidence pyramid in medical research shows (Fig. 1.1) that the best evidence is systematic reviews, which summarize previously conducted research with a higher sample size. This allows for the discovery of knowledge gaps and result summaries.

Currently, most researchers conduct systematic reviews as a part of their thesis, postdoc fellowship education, or research training program.

During conducting a systematic review, researchers learn how to develop a structured review question, register the review protocol in related databases, critique the previous findings, synthesize results, and make recommendations for future research.

FIGURE 1.1

Evidence pyramid in medical research.

Why did we write this book?

Many books are available in the field of systematic review and meta-analysis. Still, most of them lack step-by-step instructions on conducting a systematic review and, if possible, meta-analysis. They also do not follow specific examples during the book journey.

This book will provide step-by-step methods for conducting a systematic review and meta-analysis using specific examples. Also, we will introduce different software for meta-analysis, present network meta-analysis, and discuss ethical issues of systematic reviews. We also will talk about the scientific writing of systematic reviews, which will help researchers prepare their manuscripts appropriately and scientifically.

Research methodology: Primary versus secondary studies

2

Mahsa Ghajarzadeh and Margaret Vieira

Department of Neurology, Johns Hopkins University School of Medicine, Baltimore, MD, United States

Introduction

Study design is the set of methods and techniques that are used to conduct a research study (acquiring information, data analysis, and reporting of final results). There are different types of study design, and each design has its own advantages and disadvantages which we will discuss throughout this chapter [1].

To determine the most appropriate study design, we have to know the research question and study's goal, as well as our resources and the budget. It is essential to keep in mind that study design ensures the validity of the findings (external validity) and the application of the results in clinical practice.

Research studies can be either primary or secondary. Primary research is based on data we have gathered throughout the study from participants, while secondary research is based on primary data sources that were collected for another purposes [1,2].

Types of studies

Generally, we categorize research studies into two main types: observational studies and interventional studies.

The researcher does not implement an intervention for study participants in observational studies. The researchers only observes the relationship between exposure and outcome in observational studies [3].

The researcher would implement an intervention as part of the study design in interventional studies such as trials.

We summarized types of studies in a diagram (Fig. 2.1).

Systematic Review and Meta-Analysis. https://doi.org/10.1016/B978-0-443-13428-9.00002-1

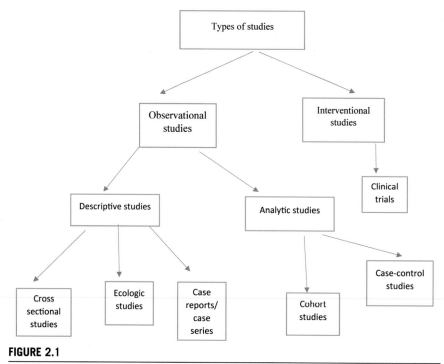

FIGURE 2.1

Flow diagram of the different types of studies.

Observational studies
Case reports/case series

A case series study describes the characteristics of a group of people with the same disease, or exposure. In this type of descriptive study, we report demographics, disease presentation(s), prognosis, survival,... of individuals with a particular disease or exposure that is not common or well-known [4].

A case report is the description of a single case.

Case reports and case series influence medical literature by advancing the knowledge of rare or new diseases, their presentations, and side effects [3].

Advantages of reporting a case or cases:

1. Introducing new diseases, new symptoms, or signs,
2. Describing rare adverse effects, newly found effects of a specific treatment,
3. Introducing the mechanism of the disease.

Disadvantages:

1. No statistical analysis,
2. No conclusions can be made (no inference or any associations),
3. An extensive number of observations are needed.

Example:

1. Guillain–Barré syndrome following different COVID-19 vaccines: a case series [5]. In this study, authors highlighted the incidence of GBS after COVID-19 vaccines in seven cases. Each of the seven subjects had an age range of between 29 and 59 years.
2. Post-COVID factor x deficiency: A case report from Pakistan [6].
   In this study, authors described a 38-year-old man who had factor X deficiency after COVID-19 infection.

Ecologic studies

In this type of observational studies, measurements are taken on a group of people not on individual subjects. These measurements can be performed on a small group, such as people living within a particular home, or they can be performed on a large group, such as the population living within a specific country or continent. This type of study can be used to report the health issues of different populations such as the COVID-19 infection rates in various countries or continents [7]. The only disadvantage of this type of study is the inability to generalize the results to any specific individual. If the results are applied to any specific individual, this is called an ecologic fallacy. This type of study has its advantages and disadvantages:

Advantages of ecologic studies:

1. They are not costly,
2. They provide information regarding a specific group of people,
3. They are suitable for health policy studies.

Disadvantages of ecologic studies:

1. Results cannot be generalized and applied to each individual in a specific group,
2. The results of one group cannot be generalized and applied to another group.

To overcome the ecologic fallacy, you can combine ecological- and individual-level data [7].

Examples:

Environmental air pollution and acute cerebrovascular complications: an ecologic study in Tehran, Iran [8].

In this study, the authors included 1491 patients' diagnosis with stroke in eight referral hospitals in different regions of Tehran (the capital of Iran). The researchers measured daily average levels of varying air pollutants, including CO, NO(X), SO [2], O(3), and PM(10) on the day the stroke occurred and 48 h before the day of the stroke.

Cross-sectional studies

Cross-sectional studies are known as prevalence studies and are designed to estimate the prevalence of the outcome of interest in a specific population [9]. These studies provide a snapshot of the desired outcome at a specific time.

Cross-sectional studies cannot be used for causality purposes as they are performed at one specific time point and do not give any sequential information of the events. The main concern about this type of study is the representativeness of the findings, as method of sampling plays a vital role in the generalizability of the results [9].

Advantages of a cross-sectional study:

1. Estimates the prevalence of the disease(s) or targeted situation,
2. Need less cost and time,
3. Cross-sectional studies are useful for public health surveys,
4. Cross-sectional studies provide opportunities for planning prospective studies,
5. We can assess many outcomes and risk factors at the same time by conducting cross-sectional studies [9,10].

Disadvantages of a cross-sectional study:

1. We cannot derive a causal relationship by conducting this type of study, as exposures and outcomes are measured at the same time
2. By conducting the same cross-sectional study at a different time frame, different results may be obtained by conducting the same cross-sectional study at a different time-frame

Examples:

A. Prevalence of multiple sclerosis (MS) disease in one of the cities (Zanjan) in Iran (prevalence of MS in Zanjan Province of Iran) [11].
B. The effects of air pollution on vitamin D status in healthy women: A cross-sectional study [12].

Case-control studies

Case-control design is one of the fundamental study designs to detect the associations between exposures and outcomes.

These studies need less time, money, and effort, and study groups are defined based on the outcome of interest, rather than the exposure [13]. Hence, this type of studies is considered to be a retrospective research study, as we recruit patients, and controls and seek for their exposures in the past (Fig. 2.2).

FIGURE 2.2

Case-control studies.

In case-control studies, researchers look back in time to detect each individual's exposure status, which makes case-control studies prone to recall bias (some participants remember nonrelevant events as exposure, and others do not remember the real exposure).

The two main concerns regarding case-control studies are choosing the best controls for the cases and accurately determining the exposure history in both case and control groups.

Controls should be similar to cases in many ways and at analogous risk of developing the outcome during that time [14].

Strengths of a case-control study

1. Case-control studies are inexpensive and cost effective,
2. They need less time and effort,
3. Case-control studies show causal associations,
4. They can find multiple risk factors for a specific outcome.

Limitations of case-control studies

1. The selection of proper controls is a pertinent issue,
2. Matching cases and controls for potential confounders should be considered,
3. They are prone to a wide range of biases, especially recall bias,
4. The retrospective nature of the case-control studies makes application of the results difficult.

Example:

If you want to find the potential risk factors of pancreatic cancer, you may have a group of patients with pancreatic cancer with age- and sex-matched controls to explore their previous dietary habits as risk factors for developing pancreatic cancer.

(Dietary patterns associated with the risk of pancreatic cancer case-control study findings) [15].

Cohort studies

Cohort studies or incidence studies are studies that subjects are followed over a specific time period. These observational studies are applied to assess the causal relationships between exposures and outcomes [16]. Cohort studies can be fixed during the duration of the study (subjects would not be replaced, even if they dropout) or dynamic (recruiting new subjects when a subject is dropped out).

There are two main types of cohort studies: retrospective and prospective.

Prospective cohort studies

In this type of cohort studies, subjects who are exposed to certain risk factors are followed from the beginning of the study (this can be either in the present or future) to the end of study time period.

This follow-up requires money, time, effort, and precision to accurately detect outcomes of interest. Lost to follow-up is another disadvantage of these types of studies.

Retrospective cohort studies

In retrospective cohort studies, we look back at the previous medical records of the subjects and their follow up for a specific period of time in order to record the outcome(s) of interest.

Comparing to prospective cohort studies, retrospective cohort studies require less money, time, staff, and effort. The main disadvantage of retrospective studies is that reliance on the information gathered should be done cautiously [16].

The timelines of different cohort studies are shown in Fig. 2.3.

Strengths of cohort studies

1. Identification of a causal relationship between exposure and outcomes,
2. More than one outcome for specific exposures can be identified,
3. The incidence of the outcome of interest can be measured.

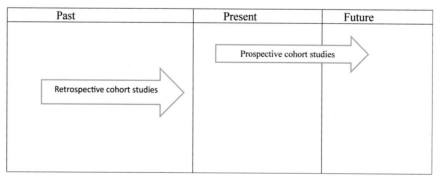

FIGURE 2.3

The timelines of different cohort studies.

Limitations of cohort studies

1. Taking more time, cost, and effort,
2. In retrospective cohort studies, a precise record of exposures is desirable,
3. Prospective cohort studies are prone to the loss to follow-up,
4. If the outcome of interest is rare, a large sample size is required.

Examples:

1. Framingham heart study was a prospective cohort study, which included 5209 women and men with an age range of 30–62 years [17,18]. They followed the included individuals to see how cardiovascular health affects the body.
2. The Dutch famine birth cohort study was a retrospective cohort study including 1116 female children who were born in Amsterdam during Hunger Winter [19]. Adults who were in utero in at the end of World War II had a wide range of physical and mental health problems as their mothers experienced food shortages due to the Nazi regime.

Interventional studies

Interventional studies are studies in which researchers perform an intervention on a group of people and evaluate their outcomes on disease progression, level of biomarkers, radiological findings, level of disability, and patient reported outcomes.

Uncontrolled clinical trials, nonrandomized controlled trials, and randomized clinical trials (RCTs) are the three main types of interventional studies.

The most critical interventional studies are RCTs, which are considered to be the gold standard for efficacy evaluations [20]. In these studies, potential participants are randomly assigned into either intervention or control groups and will be followed-up for a specific time period. At the end of follow up, outcomes of interest will be evaluated.

In an ideal RCT design, neither the researcher nor the participants are aware of assignment groups. This is called blinding, which helps better controlling of potential biases and ensures precise assessment.

RCTs have four phases which are summarized in Table 2.1 [21].

Advantages of RCTs

1. Good evidence of causality,
2. By performing randomization, both groups have the same chance of receiving the intervention,
3. Trials provide the best evidence of efficacy and also side effects of specific medications.

Table 2.1 Four phases of RCTs.

Phase	Objective	Typical no. of patients
I	Explore and determine the toxic effects, and also tolerance of the intervention	10 to 30
II	Evaluating the therapeutic effect of the intervention and also the risks.	20 to 50
III	Comparing the new treatment to standard of care treatment or a control population or placebo	100 to 1000
IV	To obtain a large amount of information regarding morbidity or late side effects	Hundreds/Thousands

Disadvantages

1. Interventional studies are costly,
2. They need more staff and effort,
3. They need more participants,
4. Any error in the study design will cause errors in the results.

Examples:

1. Pilot randomized active-placebo-controlled trial of low-dose ketamine for the treatment of MS-related fatigue.

   In this clinical trial, authors enrolled 18 patients with MS and randomly assigned them into the ketamine or placebo group (midazolam). Subjects were followed for 1 month. The researchers assessed Daily Fatigue Severity (DFS) and Modified Fatigue Impact Scale (MFIS) as study outcomes [22].

Secondary studies

In primary studies, we gather original data from individual patients, while in secondary studies, we use data that already exist. We will pool and synthesize the results by using the advanced methods.

A study of studies is defined as a secondary study (for example, review of individual studies) [23]. Fourteen types of review studies are defined and are shown in Table 2.2 [24].

Table 2.2 Types of review studies.

Types of reviews
Critical review
Literature review
Mapping review
Meta-analysis
Mixed studies review/mixed methods review
Overview
Qualitative systematic review/qualitative evidence synthesis
Rapid review
Scoping review
State-of-the-art review
Systematic review
Systematic search and review
Systematized review
Umbrella review

Two most common review studies are narrative reviews, and systematic reviews.

Narrative reviews

The terms systematic review, and narrative review are often mistakenly used synonymously, but they are totally different. An expert in the field is asked to write a comprehensive review on a topic, by reading relevant studies, then summarizing (not mathematically) the findings, and concluding the main findings to provide a narrative review in the field. This type of reviews provides an overview of the topic at hand, but it is prone to a wide range of biases based on the writer's expertise, his/her own findings in the field, and potential conflicts of interest. Some common concerns with narrative reviews are the lack of a well-defined question (they are subjective), the shortage of a comprehensive literature search, no definite review strategy, as well as the absence of a quality assessment of included studies that are fundamentals of a systematic review.

Systematic reviews are team-based studies, and researchers answer a specific question through a comprehensive search.

Comparing with a narrative review, a systematic review has the following discrete steps:

A: Identify a specific question
B. Write and register study protocol, including a prespecified search strategy and study quality assessment.

C. Perform a systematic and comprehensive literature review
D. Screen titles and abstracts
E. Obtain full texts of studies identified in step D
F. Select relevant studies
G. Extract data
H. Perform quality assessment of included studies
I. Summarize the results and if possible, synthesize the data
J. Write a manuscript describing systematic review's findings, and submit it for publication to the scientific community

Advantages of narrative reviews:

1. Provides an overview of a particular topic
2. Covers a wide range of issues within a given topic.

Disadvantages of narrative reviews:

1. No statistical analysis is performed
2. They are opinion-based studies
3. They are susceptible to reviewers' bias
4. The researchers doing this type of review do not perform a quality assessment of the included studies

Examples:

1. Kidney injury associated with COVID-19 infection and vaccine: A narrative review

In this article authors summarize the kidney injuries associated with COVID-19 or its vaccines, the mechanism, clinical findings, and outcomes.

In the next chapters, we will focus on systematic reviews and conducting them step by step.

References

[1] Petitti DB. Meta-analysis, decision analysis and cost-effectiveness analysis. Methods for quantitative synthesis in medicine. Monogr Epidemiol Biostat 1994;24:119—23.
[2] Sutton AJ, Abrams KR, Jones DR, Jones DR, Sheldon TA, Song F. Methods for meta-analysis in medical research. Chichester: Wiley; 2000.
[3] Murad MH, Sultan S, Haffar S, Bazerbachi F. Methodological quality and synthesis of case series and case reports. BMJ evidence-based medicine 2018;23(2):60—3.
[4] Vandenbroucke JP. In defense of case reports and case series. Annals of internal medicine 2001;134(4):330—4.
[5] Shalash A, Belal N, Zaki AS, Georgy SS, Doheim MF, Hazzou A, et al. Guillain—Barré syndrome following different COVID-19 vaccines: a case series. The Egyptian Journal of Neurology. Psychiatry and Neurosurgery 2022;58(1):1—6.

[6] Humayun O, Durrani T, Ullah R, Qayum I, Khan MI, ijaz Khan M. Post-COVID factor X deficiency: a case report from Pakistan. Cureus 2022;14(11).

[7] Wakefield J. Ecologic studies revisited. Annu Rev Public Health 2008;29:75−90.

[8] Nabavi SM, Jafari B, Jalali MS, Nedjat S, Ashrafi K, Salahesh A. Environmental air pollution and acute cerebrovascular complications: an ecologic study in Tehran, Iran. Int J Prev Med 2012;3(10):723.

[9] Levin KA. Study design III: cross-sectional studies. Evid Base Dent 2006;7(1):24−5.

[10] Setia MS. Methodology series module 3: cross-sectional studies. Indian J Dermatol 2016;61(3):261.

[11] Ghajarzadeh M, Foroushani AR, Ghezelbash P, Ghoreishi A, Maghbooli M, Yousefi M, et al. Prevalence of multiple sclerosis (MS) in Zanjan Province of Iran. Int J Prev Med 2020;11:116.

[12] Hosseinpanah F, Heibatollahi M, Moghbel N, Asefzade S, Azizi F. The effects of air pollution on vitamin D status in healthy women: a cross sectional study. BMC Publ Health 2010;10(1):1−6.

[13] Schulz KF, Grimes DA. Case-control studies: research in reverse. The lancet 2002; 359(9304):431−4.

[14] Lewallen S, Courtright P. Epidemiology in practice: case-control studies. Community Eye Health 1998;11(28):57.

[15] Tayyem R, Hammad S, Allehdan S, Al-Jaberi T, Hushki A, Rayyan Y, et al. Dietary patterns associated with the risk of pancreatic cancer: case-control study findings. Medicine 2022;101(48):e31886.

[16] Levin KA. Study design IV: cohort studies. Evid Base Dent 2006;7(2):51−2.

[17] Manson JE, Bassuk SS. Invited Commentary: the framingham offspring study—a pioneering investigation into familial aggregation of cardiovascular risk. Am J Epidemiol 2017;185(11):1103−8.

[18] Bitton A, Gaziano T. The Framingham Heart Study's impact on global risk assessment. Prog Cardiovasc Dis 2010;53(1):68−78.

[19] Lumey LH, Ravelli AC, Wiessing LG, Koppe JG, Treffers PE, Stein ZA. The Dutch famine birth cohort study: design, validation of exposure, and selected characteristics of subjects after 43 years follow-up. Paediatr Perinat Epidemiol 1993;7(4):354−67.

[20] Spieth PM, Kubasch AS, Penzlin AI, Illigens BM-W, Barlinn K, Siepmann T. Randomized controlled trials—a matter of design. Neuropsychiatric Dis Treat 2016;12:1341.

[21] Stanley K. Design of randomized controlled trials. Circulation 2007;115(9):1164−9.

[22] Fitzgerald KC, Morris B, Soroosh A, Balshi A, Maher D, Kaplin A, et al. Pilot randomized active-placebo-controlled trial of low-dose ketamine for the treatment of multiple sclerosis-related fatigue. Mult Scler 2021;27(6):942−53.

[23] Garousi V, Mäntylä MV. A systematic literature review of literature reviews in software testing. Inf Software Technol 2016;80:195−216.

[24] Grant MJ, Booth A. A typology of reviews: an analysis of 14 review types and associated methodologies. Health information & libraries journal 2009;26(2):91−108.

Why do we need systematic reviews?

3

Mahsa Ghajarzadeh and Kathryn C. Fitzgerald

Department of Neurology, Johns Hopkins University School of Medicine, Baltimore, MD, United States

There are a number of reasons that show the need for new systematic reviews in the field of medical research. Systematic reviews are essential pieces of evidence for clinicians, researchers, policy-makers, and governments.

Healthcare providers are flooded with uncontrollable amounts of information, so they need systematic reviews to integrate available information in the best way and apply them for decision-making [1]. Systematic reviews also provide information regarding the generalizability of scientific findings of previous research regarding different characteristics of various populations.

For many researchers, clinicians, policy-makers, and governments, it is not possible to read, critically appraise, and apply the best evidence by themselves. This method needs knowledge, expertise, and also time.

Systematic reviews are a popular type of secondary studies. The goal of systematic reviews is to provide an evidence-based answer to a detailed inquiry that is completed using a comprehensive and systematic literature search that is followed by an appraisal and synthesis of the evidence.

The rationales for conducting systematic reviews are listed below:

1. Systematic reviews reduce a large amount of information into palatable pieces.
2. Systematic reviews can establish the generalizability of scientific findings.
3. Sometimes, conducting a systematic review is less costly and timely of conducting new original research.
4. Systematic reviews are helpful in assessing the consistency of the relationships between variables.
5. Systematic review (if they are done properly) is accurate and reflects the reality in the field.
6. As the steps of conducting systematic reviews are clear, replication of systematic reviews is possible and they could be assessed very simply [1].

We can go through the example. A 38-year-old woman who has consumed oral contraceptive pills (OCPs) for more than 10 years is worried about developing multiple sclerosis (MS) during life. She asks her gynecologists about her question. The doctor can search databases and find confusing results. Some studies revealed that OCPs increase the risk of developing MS, while others not. Back in the library

Systematic Review and Meta-Analysis. https://doi.org/10.1016/B978-0-443-13428-9.00003-3

and finding a systematic review and meta-analysis for this case, the doctor will ensure the patient that she is not at higher risk for developing MS comparing to whom have not use OCPs [2].

The results of a systematic review help researchers and clinicians reach conclusions related to a defined question and can provide a level of confidence in the conclusion, underscoring whether further research is needed [3]. Systematic reviews are also important for highlighting gaps in knowledge that can help direct and plan subsequent studies aimed at addressing these gaps.

Systematic reviews sit at the top of the medical evidence pyramid, followed by clinical trials, cohort studies, case control studies, etc [4]. This position indicates that systematic reviews provide high level of evidence although there not lots of them [5] (Fig. 3.1).

Systematic reviews have major advantages:

(1) Answering a specific question
(2) Increasing precision and power; many individual studies have small sample sizes and combination of all relevant studies acts to increase the overall sample size and can help refine effect estimates, thereby increasing power and precision
(3) Objectively appraisal of the evidence thus contributing to resolve the uncertainty
(4) Resolving controversies
(5) Identifying gaps in knowledge
(6) No need for ethics committee approval or approval from other regulatory bodies
(7) No need consent of the patients [6]

FIGURE 3.1

Evidence pyramid in medical research.

The most important advantage of a systematic review is transparency of review process, which makes repetition possible.

A good systematic review should focus on a well-defined question and uses appropriate methods, following comprehensive search in relevant databases (at least four databases), applying definite criteria for including studies, quality assessment, and finally data synthesis.

If all steps are not well specified and documented, results and conclusions will not be confidential.

After defining your specific question, we recommend the systematic review protocol is written and registered in relevant databases.

This registration will provide the advantages of giving information regarding ongoing systematic reviews to others, preventing reworking, and provide transparency [7]. As this process requires an investigator to delineate their search strategy, it also helps them scope out possible searches and provides an estimate of the time and personnel needed to complete the review. In addition, delineating the review question, inclusion, and exclusion criteria, search strategy, data extraction, method of quality assessment, and plans for data synthesis is extremely helpful for the final step of drafting and submitting the manuscript.

We recommend PROSPERO for protocol registration; it is user-friendly and registration is generally seamless and not time-consuming (Fig. 3.2).

If you wish to conduct a systematic review of the effect of the health intervention, we recommend you to search Database of Abstracts of Reviews of Effects (DARE) (Fig. 3.3).

PROSPERO is fast-tracking registration of protocols related to COVID-19

PROSPERO accepts registrations for systematic reviews, **rapid reviews** and umbrella reviews. PROSPERO **does not accept scoping reviews** or **literature scans**. Sibling PROSPERO sites registers systematic reviews of **human studies** and systematic reviews of **animal studies**.

Before registering a new systematic review, check **PROSPERO** and the resources on COVID-END to see whether a similar review already exists. If so, **please do not duplicate without good reason**. Your efforts may be much more useful if switched to a different topic. This will avoid research waste and contribute more effectively to tackling the pandemic.

Shortcut for **already registered** reviews of human and animal **studies** relevant to Covid-19, tagged by research area

FIGURE 3.2

PROSPERO preface.

Database of Abstracts of Reviews of Effects (DARE)

Titles	Database of Abstracts of Reviews of Effects (DARE)
Access/status	Open Access
URL	Connect to database
Description	DARE (Database of Abstracts of Reviews of Effects), located on the University of York Centre for Reviews and Dissemination platform, is an index of over 35,000 systematic reviews of health and social care interventions. These reviews evaluate the effects of health and social care interventions and the delivery and organization of health and social care services. It also indexes reviews of the wider determinants of health, such as housing and transport, in cases where these impact health or have the potential to impact health and wellbeing.
	DARE does not contain the full text of reviews; rather, it contains indexing, citations, and abstracts for reviews. In some cases, it includes a link to the original review. These links have not been configured for Rutgers access.
	The U.K. Department of Health and the National Institute for Health Research (NIHR) funded the production of DARE between 1994 and March 2015. The DARE records produced during this time are

Activate Windows
Go to Settings to activate

FIGURE 3.3

Database of abstracts of reviews of effects (DARE) preface.

After doing preliminary search and confirming your review question, you can go through the Critical Appraisal Skills Programme (CASP) worksheets and see what items you are asked to consider during your review (Table 3.1) [8].

This table will help you clarify your question, determine the type of studies that you want to include, determine your quality of bias evaluation, outcomes of interest to consider, external validity of the final results, and application of the results in the community.

Table 3.1 The CASP questions for systematic reviews.

CASP appraisal questions
Did the review ask a clearly focused question?
Did the review include the right type of study?
Did the reviewers try to identify all relevant studies?
Did the reviewers assess the quality of the included studies?
If the results of the studies have been combined, was it reasonable to do so?
How are the results presented and what is the main result?
How precise are these results?
Can the results be applied to the local population?
Were all important outcomes considered?
Should policy or practice change as a result of the evidence contained in this review?

Conclusions

Systematic reviews, and if possible, systematic reviews with meta-analysis, provide higher quality evidence regarding the question. They are also valuable in providing areas, which lack evidence, and where new, high-quality studies are required.

In next chapters, we will go through systematic review steps with practical examples.

References

[1] Mulrow CD. Systematic reviews: rationale for systematic reviews. BMJ 1994;309(6954): 597—9.

[2] Ghajarzadeh M, Mohammadi A, Shahraki Z, Sahraian MA, Mohammadifar M. Pregnancy history, oral contraceptive pills consumption (OCPs), and risk of Multiple Sclerosis: a systematic review and meta-analysis. Int J Prev Med 2022;13:89.

[3] Sofaer N, Strech D. The need for systematic reviews of reasons. Bioethics 2012;26(6): 315—28.

[4] Rosner AL. Evidence-based medicine: revisiting the pyramid of priorities. J Bodyw Mov Ther 2012;16(1):42—9.

[5] https://academicguides.waldenu.edu/library/healthevidence/evidencepyramid.

[6] Wormald R, Evans J. What makes systematic reviews systematic and why are they the highest level of evidence? Taylor & Francis; 2018. p. 27—30.

[7] Page MJ, Shamseer L, Tricco AC. Registration of systematic reviews in PROSPERO: 30,000 records and counting. Syst Rev 2018;7(1):1—9.

[8] Richards D. Critically appraising systematic reviews. Evid Base Dent 2010;11(1):27—9.

Registering the protocol and structure the question

4

Mahsa Ghajarzadeh and Margaret Vieira

Department of Neurology, Johns Hopkins University School of Medicine, Baltimore, MD, United States

In Chapter 3, we explained how to select a topic properly. In this chapter, we will discuss specific parts of the review question, its details, and the registration process in PROSPERO.

We also will define a structured question, which is a fundamental part of conducting a systematic review. We will also discuss how to register the review question in PROSPERO.

The most critical phase of a systematic review is developing and refining the review question (which guides you through the systematic review process).

After determining your area of research, you can define your review question. Your question should be clear, structured, and related to your outcome of interest.

After defining the review question, you should perform a literature review to explore if the same review exists or not. If the same review is present that covers the same question as yours, explore how you can edit your review question, or what new aspect you can provide to update the previous one.

After a scoping review, you will discover how much time and staff you need to complete the review process. A scoping review is a quick noncomprehensive search that helps you scope your review process. You can rapidly search PubMed or Google Scholar. It is a must to search the Cochrane Database of Systematic Reviews (CDSR) and PROSPERO to uncover if there are any available systematic reviews or registered protocols.

After performing a scoping review, if you find that there is a similar review with the same question, and if there are no more studies to add the previous review, you should change your question.

Previously, most systematic reviews focused on trials. Currently, we have systematic reviews that are designed to estimate the pooled prevalence/incidence of various diseases or conditions, find the pooled diagnostic profile of the investigative tests, investigate the pooled causal relationship between dependent, and independent variables, and find the pooled effects of interventions.

Therefore, based on the primary outcome of your review, we can have different types of questions:

Systematic Review and Meta-Analysis. **https://doi.org/10.1016/B978-0-443-13428-9.00004-5**

Here are some examples:

1. What is the pooled prevalence of diabetes mellitus type II in Asia? (Prevalence question)
2. What is the pooled incidence of skin cancer in patients with multiple sclerosis (MS)? (Incidence question)
3. Are women of reproductive age who use oral contraceptives (OCPs) at a higher risk of developing Neuromyelitis Optica Spectrum Disorder (NMOSD) than women without OCP administration history? (Harm question)
4. Do women undergoing in vitro fertilization (IVF) benefit from vitamin D supplements compared with placebo to achieve IVF success? (Intervention question)
5. How good is sonoelastography for differentiating benign and malignant thyroid nodules? (Diagnostic question)

Each type of question requires a different type of studies to minimize bias. The standard format of systematic review questions is PICO, which is defined as:

A. Patients (population),
B. Intervention,
C. Comparator,
D. Outcome.

This format works for systematic reviews that plan to assess the effects of an intervention in comparison with a control (maybe placebo).

1. Do women undergoing in vitro fertilization (IVF) (**P**) benefit from vitamin D supplements (**I**) compared with placebo (**C**) to achieve IVF outcomes (**O**)?

Some researchers add "TS" to their question:

T: Timing (duration of treatment, duration of follow up …),
S: Setting (inpatients, outpatient …).

For systematic reviews where we plan to assess the association between an exposure, and a definite outcome, we can use the PECO format:

A. Patients (population),
B. Exposure,
C. Comparator (optional),
D. Outcome.

An investigator can register their protocol through different websites such as:

1. Cochrane Database of Systematic Reviews (CDSR) (8) (Fig. 4.1),
2. PROSPERO (**Prospective Register of Systematic Reviews**) (9).
   Before registering an investigator registers their protocol, they can search the database to confirm similar protocols are not registered, which can help to avoid duplication of efforts at an early stage.

FIGURE 4.1

Cochrane library search for reviews.

3. Are women of reproductive age (**P**) who use oral contraceptives (**E**) for at least 1 year at a higher risk of developing Neuromyelitis Optica Spectrum Disorder (NMOSD) (**O**)?

For exposures, it is better to define timing of exposure, route of exposure, dose intensity, and duration of exposure.

After defining your review question, write your review protocol that includes details of your proposed research activity during the conduction of the systematic review.

Protocols include a structured question, search strategy, databases for literature search, inclusion and exclusion criteria, data extraction time frame, quality assessment scale, the staff involve, and more [1].

By registering your protocol, you create a record of what is going to be done, and you may cite the registration code in the method section of the final manuscript. We recommend you register your protocol in PROSPERO, a user friendly and easy to navigate database.

What is prospective register of systematic reviews [2]?

PROSPERO is an international database designed to register the protocol of the systematic review involving a health related outcome [1]. Checking available records help to avoid duplication, and saves time as you proceed with completing your review (as you can come back and reference your assumed tasks).

You can access PROSPERO through:

https://www.crd.york.ac.uk/PROSPERO/

On the first page, you can search for registered protocols to find if there are any similar ones (Fig. 4.2).

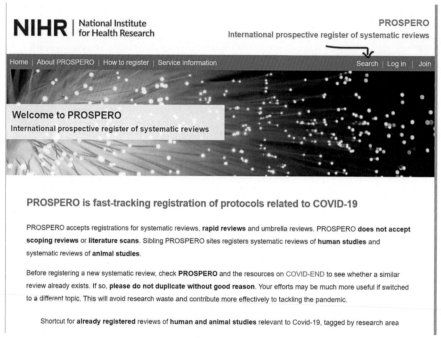

FIGURE 4.2

Search option in PROSPERO.

To register your protocol, you should have a profile in PROSPERO. You should sign up on the website and then continue registering your protocol.

On the main page of PROSPERO, you can register by clicking 'Join' on the green toolbar (Fig. 4.3).

After logging in, you can go to My PROSPER to register your protocol.

After clicking 'My PROSPER' icon, two additional icons will appear: Register your review now, and Edit your details.

By clicking on 'Register your review now', you will proceed through the registration steps based on the title of your review (animal or human-related systematic review) (Fig. 4.4):

If your title includes 'health research studies', you will be asked to answer additional questions. After completing the previous steps, you can proceed with registering your protocol.

All sections with an asterisk are mandatory

Primarily, you are asked to enter the title, the start and completion dates (Fig. 4.5).

Then, you should define the review stage, and list the primary contact person's name (Fig. 4.6).

All review team members should be registered, and funding sources should be clarified (Fig. 4.7).

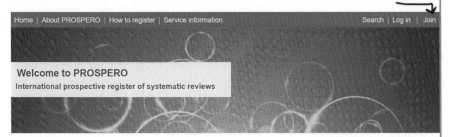

PROSPERO is fast-tracking registration of protocols related to COVID-19

PROSPERO accepts registrations for systematic reviews, **rapid reviews** and umbrella reviews. PROSPERO **does not accept scoping reviews** or **literature scans**. Sibling PROSPERO sites registers systematic reviews of **human studies** and systematic reviews of **animal studies**.

Before registering a new systematic review, check **PROSPERO** and the resources on COVID-END to see whether a similar review already exists. If so, **please do not duplicate without good reason**. Your efforts may be much more useful if switched to a different topic. This will avoid research waste and contribute more effectively to tackling the pandemic.

Shortcut for **already registered** reviews of **human and animal studies** relevant to Covid-19, tagged by research area

FIGURE 4.3

The join bottom for registering in PROSPERO.

Registering a review is easy. Please read the guidance notes for registering a **systematic review of human studies** or a **systematic review of animal studies relevant to human health**, then just follow the five step process below.

Step 1   Check the **inclusion criteria** to make sure that your review is eligible for inclusion in PROSPERO

Step 2   Ensure that your review protocol is in its (near) final form and that no major changes are anticipated at this stage - e.g. if your protocol will be peer reviewed it will usually be sensible to wait until this is complete before registering.

Step 3   Search PROSPERO to ensure that your review has not already been registered by another member of your team

Step 4   Search PROSPERO to ensure that you are not unnecessarily duplicating a review that is being done by another team or has been registered previously

Step 5   Start registering your review

 Register a systematic review of health research studies (**study participants are people**)   Register a systematic review of animal research studies (**study subjects are animals**) that is of direct relevance to human health

FIGURE 4.4

Selecting between human or animal protocol registration.

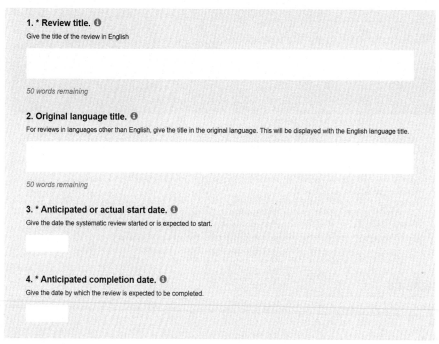

FIGURE 4.5

Title and date registration.

5. * Stage of review at time of this submission. ⓘ

This field uses answers to initial screening questions. It cannot be edited until after registration.

Tick the boxes to show which review tasks have been started and which have been completed.

Update this field each time any amendments are made to a published record.

☑ The review has not yet started

Review stage	Started	Completed
Preliminary searches	☐	☐
Piloting of the study selection process	☐	☐
Formal screening of search results against eligibility criteria	☐	☐
Data extraction	☐	☐
Risk of bias (quality) assessment	☐	☐
Data analysis	☐	☐

Provide any other relevant information about the stage of the review here.

6. * Named contact. ⓘ

The named contact is the guarantor for the accuracy of the information in the register record. This may be any member of the review team.

Email salutation (e.g. "Dr Smith" or "Joanne") for correspondence:

FIGURE 4.6

Ongoing registration.

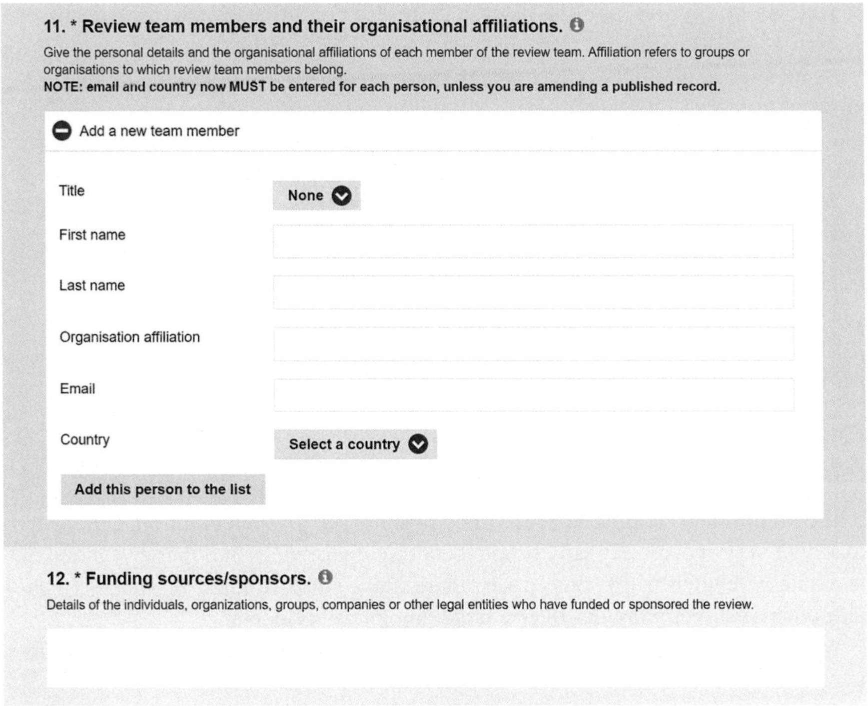

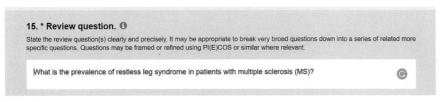

11. * **Review team members and their organisational affiliations.** ⓘ

Give the personal details and the organisational affiliations of each member of the review team. Affiliation refers to groups or organisations to which review team members belong.
NOTE: email and country now MUST be entered for each person, unless you are amending a published record.

⊖ Add a new team member

Title   None ⌄

First name

Last name

Organisation affiliation

Email

Country   Select a country ⌄

Add this person to the list

12. * **Funding sources/sponsors.** ⓘ

Details of the individuals, organizations, groups, companies or other legal entities who have funded or sponsored the review.

FIGURE 4.7

Registration of review members, and defining funding sources.

Item 15 in PROSPERO is a review question box, which asks you to enter your review question based on PICO or another proper format (Fig. 4.8).

After defining your review question, you should clearly describe your inclusion and exclusion criteria.

For example, do you want to include all patients with MS, or do you want to include cases with a definite type of the disease?

There are separate boxes for defining the details of the review question in PROSPERO.

15. * **Review question.** ⓘ

State the review question(s) clearly and precisely. It may be appropriate to break very broad questions down into a series of related more specific questions. Questions may be framed or refined using PI(E)COS or similar where relevant.

What is the prevalence of restless leg syndrome in patients with multiple sclerosis (MS)?   ↻

FIGURE 4.8

Entering review question.

You can briefly describe the disease or health condition you wish to focus on (Section 18 in PROSPERO) (Fig. 4.9).

As mentioned previously, the population of interest should be clearly defined. Do you want to include all patients with MS or patients with a definite type of the disease, or do you want to limit your review to patients with a disease duration of fewer than 5 years or not (Fig. 4.10)?

When defining the population, based on your question, you could consider these items:

A. The exact definition of the population,
B. The most essential characteristics of the patients,
C. Relevant demographic factors,
D. Settings (inpatient, out-patient …),
E. Diagnostic criteria,
F. The exact exclusion criteria,
G. Possibility of considering only a subset of the patients.

The preliminary scoping review will help you to set your intervention, either very broadly or very specifically (any supplement therapy or vitamin d therapy) based on the available evidence. In some cases, there are a small number of studies in the field; otherwise, you may discover a large amount of evidence.

When performing a comparative study, you should clearly define the comparators (placebos, vitamin d injection vs. supplements) (Fig. 4.11).

In the next section, you should define the type of studies you want to include. The reliability of the results and validity of the pooled estimates mainly depend on the type of included studies.

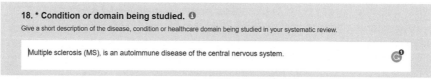

18. * Condition or domain being studied.
Give a short description of the disease, condition or healthcare domain being studied in your systematic review.

Multiple sclerosis (MS), is an autoimmune disease of the central nervous system.

FIGURE 4.9

Defining the condition of interest.

19. * Participants/population.
Specify the participants or populations being studied in the review. The preferred format includes details of both inclusion and exclusion criteria.

Patients with any type of MS disease.

FIGURE 4.10

Defining the population.

20. * Intervention(s), exposure(s). ⓘ

Give full and clear descriptions or definitions of the interventions or the exposures to be reviewed. The preferred format includes details of both inclusion and exclusion criteria.

200 words remaining

21. * Comparator(s)/control. ⓘ

Where relevant, give details of the alternatives against which the intervention/exposure will be compared (e.g. another intervention or a non-exposed control group). The preferred format includes details of both inclusion and exclusion criteria.

FIGURE 4.11

Defining the intervention and comparison.

For this question, we need to extract data regarding the prevalence of RLS in patients with MS. We will include cross-sectional studies, and the primary outcome will be the number of patients with RLS among patients with MS who were enrolled at the beginning of the study.

Outcome: The main outcomes that you wish to focus on should be clearly defined (Fig. 4.12).

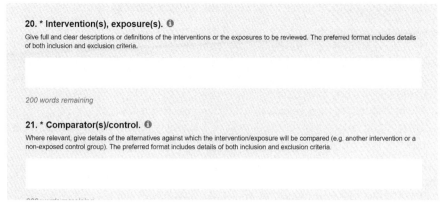

22. * Types of study to be included. ⓘ

Give details of the study designs (e.g. RCT) that are eligible for inclusion in the review. The preferred format includes both inclusion and exclusion criteria. If there are no restrictions on the types of study, this should be stated.

Cross-sectional studies.

148 words remaining

23. Context. ⓘ

Give summary details of the setting or other relevant characteristics, which help define the inclusion or exclusion criteria.

250 words remaining

24. * Main outcome(s). ⓘ

Give the pre-specified main (most important) outcomes of the review, including details of how the outcome is defined and measured and when these measurement are made, if these are part of the review inclusion criteria.

The number of patients with RLS among patients with MS who were enrolled at the beginning of the study.

FIGURE 4.12

Defining the type of study and main outcomes of interest.

If possible, you can consider five elements for each outcome:

A. Domain (for example RLS, or depression, or anxiety),
B. Specific measurement (Restless Legs Syndrome Diagnostic Index for RLS, or Beck depression inventory (BDI), or Beck anxiety Inventory (BAI)),
C. Specific metrics (for example for continuous variables change from the baseline),
D. Method of aggregation (mean, mean difference, frequency …),
E. Time period (after 3 months or 6 weeks or 3 weeks from the start of the treatment …).

Each review may have more than one outcome, but the main and primary outcome should be clearly defined (Fig. 4.13).

If the review aims to assess multiple outcomes, the inclusion and exclusion criteria should be set for the primary outcome. Restricting studies to all desired results is impossible.

The method of including studies should be clarified, and the data which are planned to be excluded from the studies should be written in details (Fig. 4.14).

Based on the types of included studies, you will use a risk of bias assessment tool (quality assessment). It should be noted that all studies with the same basic design, need to be well-conducted, but in reality, it is impossible. So, quality assessment is essential. The quality of included studies will affect the validity of the final results.

You should provide details in the dedicated box (Fig. 4.15).

Examples: Cochrane Risk of Bias Tool for Randomized Controlled Trials,

or NEWCASTLE−OTTAWA QUALITY ASSESSMENT SCALE for CASE CONTROL STUDIES,

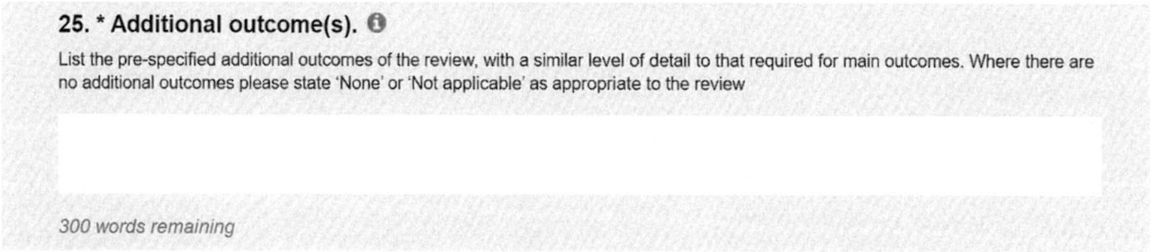

25. * Additional outcome(s). ℹ️

List the pre-specified additional outcomes of the review, with a similar level of detail to that required for main outcomes. Where there are no additional outcomes please state 'None' or 'Not applicable' as appropriate to the review

300 words remaining

FIGURE 4.13

Defining the additional outcomes.

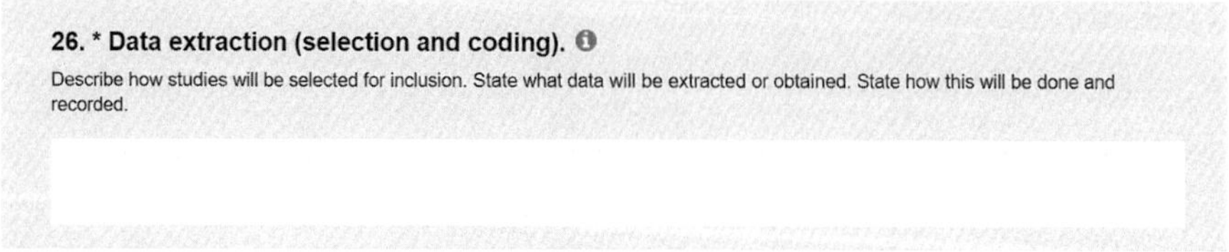

26. * Data extraction (selection and coding). ℹ️

Describe how studies will be selected for inclusion. State what data will be extracted or obtained. State how this will be done and recorded.

FIGURE 4.14

Data extraction section.

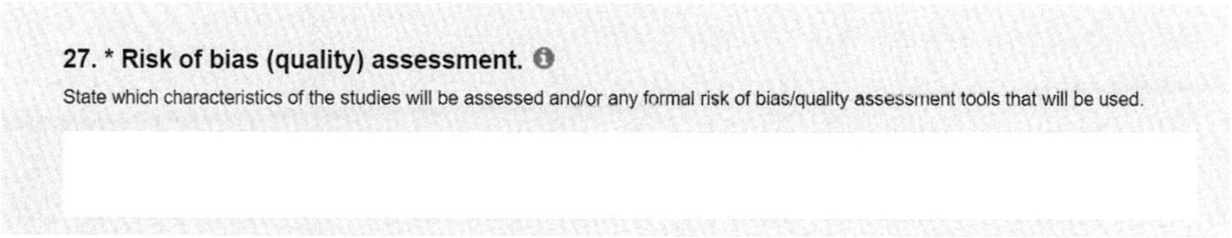

> **27. * Risk of bias (quality) assessment.** 🛈
>
> State which characteristics of the studies will be assessed and/or any formal risk of bias/quality assessment tools that will be used.

FIGURE 4.15

Risk of bias assessment section.

or NEWCASTLE–OTTAWA QUALITY ASSESSMENT SCALE for COHORT STUDIES,

or NEWCASTLE–OTTAWA QUALITY ASSESSMENT SCALE for CROSS-SECTIONAL studies.

Before concluding your systematic review, you should explore the method of data synthesis, also statistical heterogeneity assessment. The method of data synthesis should be based type of the extracted data, and planned outcomes (Fig. 4.16).

If you plan to perform subgroup analysis, specify the type of subgroup analysis in your protocol (examples: subgroup analysis based on age groups, gender, types of the disease, socioeconomic status, the disease stages) (Fig. 4.17).

The next mandatory step is to select the type and method of the systematic review (Fig. 4.18).

The country or countries of affiliated persons should be selected (Fig. 4.19).

The final mandatory step is defining the status of the review (Fig. 4.20).

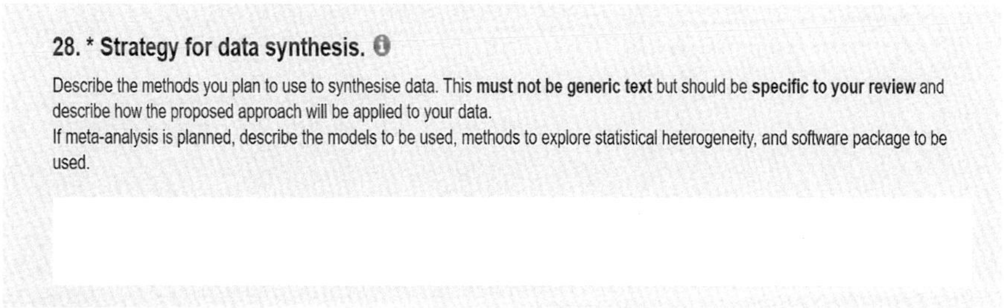

> **28. * Strategy for data synthesis.** 🛈
>
> Describe the methods you plan to use to synthesise data. This **must not be generic text** but should be **specific to your review** and describe how the proposed approach will be applied to your data.
>
> If meta-analysis is planned, describe the models to be used, methods to explore statistical heterogeneity, and software package to be used.

FIGURE 4.16

Data synthesis section.

> **29. * Analysis of subgroups or subsets.** 🛈
>
> State any planned investigation of 'subgroups'. Be clear and specific about which type of study or participant will be included in each group or covariate investigated. State the planned analytic approach.

FIGURE 4.17

Clarifying subgroup analysis.

30. * Type and method of review. ℹ

Select the type of review, review method and health area from the lists below.

Type of review

☐ Cost effectiveness

☐ Diagnostic

☐ Epidemiologic

☐ Individual patient data (IPD) meta-analysis

☐ Intervention

☐ Living systematic review

☐ Meta-analysis

☐ Methodology

☐ Narrative synthesis

☐ Network meta-analysis

☐ Pre-clinical

☐ Prevention

☐ Prognostic

☐ Prospective meta-analysis (PMA)

☐ Review of reviews

☐ Service delivery

☐ Synthesis of qualitative studies

☑ Systematic review

☐ Other

FIGURE 4.18

Selecting type, and method of review.

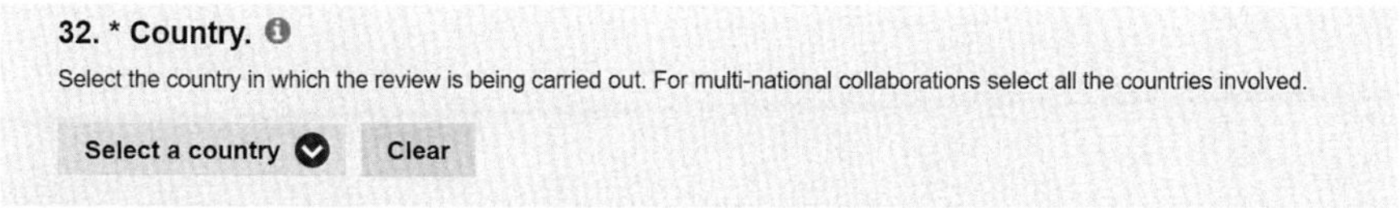

32. * Country. ⓘ

Select the country in which the review is being carried out. For multi-national collaborations select all the countries involved.

Select a country ⌄   Clear

FIGURE 4.19

Selecting the country in which the review will be done.

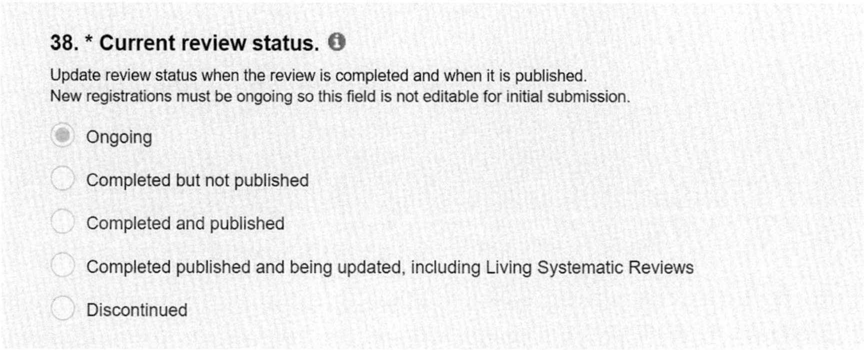

38. * Current review status. ⓘ

Update review status when the review is completed and when it is published.
New registrations must be ongoing so this field is not editable for initial submission.

◉ Ongoing

◯ Completed but not published

◯ Completed and published

◯ Completed published and being updated, including Living Systematic Reviews

◯ Discontinued

FIGURE 4.20

Defining the status of the review.

Conclusion: Defining the review question is mandatory, and recommended to be registered in a database such as PROSPERO.

References

[1] https://library.cumc.columbia.edu/insight/prospero-registry-systematic-review-protocols.
[2] https://www.crd.york.ac.uk/prospero/.

Systematic search for a systematic review

5

Mohsen Rastkar[1] and Narges Ebrahimi[2,3,4]

[1]*Tehran University of Medical Sciences, Tehran, Iran;* [2]*Department of Immunology, Faculty of Medicine, Isfahan University of Medical Sciences, Isfahan, Iran;* [3]*Immunodeficiency Diseases Research Center, Isfahan University of Medical Sciences, Isfahan, Iran;* [4]*Isfahan Neurosciences Research Center, Isfahan University of Medical Sciences, Isfahan, Iran*

Introduction

Systematic reviews require a comprehensive and sensitive search to identify all related literature and avoid bias.

To decrease bias, it is recommended to search unpublished studies, the protocols of ongoing research, conference abstracts, and references of included references.

Before conducting the main search, scoping search is recommended, which will help to improve and refine your review question, search strategy, and also clarify definition of inclusion/exclusion criteria. Using simple search terms, you can overview your review topic, and if necessary, edit your review question, and estimate how much time you need for review. For scoping search, you do not need to search all databases and read all literature.

What is a scoping search?

Scoping search is the first practical step of a systematic review, and meta-analysis. In this step, you should answer these three main questions: 1) Is this subject appropriate for a systematic review or not? 2) Is there any previous systematic review or meta-analysis on this subject? 3) Is there any registered protocol on this subject?

We usually search bibliographic databases, notably Google Scholar, and PubMed to answer the questions number one and two. Also we should search registered protocols through PROSPERO or Cochrane Library or published protocols in journals to answer question number three.

The most important advantage of this step is to help refine, and edit your review question.

Second, you can find the desired effect size, and any other essential variables that you need to work on.

Third, you can find and review previous systematic reviews in this field; so you can investigate their pros and cons to design a better study.

Systematic Review and Meta-Analysis. https://doi.org/10.1016/B978-0-443-13428-9.00005-7

Fourth, it will help you to write your protocol with a clear mind map.

Fifth, you can estimate how much time, and how many personnel you need for your review.

How should we do a scoping search?

After confirming your review topic, you can start scoping review.

For example, we are going to plan a study to find the prevalence of restless leg syndrome, among patients with multiple sclerosis (MS).

In this subject, we have two key-words, "Multiple Sclerosis" and "Restless leg syndrome". We should search syntaxes based on these two main keywords.

As it was mentioned, we open the PubMed through Medline, and type "Restless leg syndrome" AND "Multiple sclerosis" in the query box.

Notice that AND should be in capital words, multiple sclerosis should be exact in "" and Restless leg syndrome, either (See part 1.7.2.).

In a scoping search, you should not write a complex syntax with all associated terms. In this example we use "multiple sclerosis" with "Restless leg syndrome".

A scoping search should not be reported in the method section in the final manuscript.

If we find that our topic is new, or it is time to update the previous systematic review, we can establish the review question and then start the main search.

Due to the importance of the primary literature search of systematic review, in this chapter, we will show search in details in different databases for a single search question. Two independent researchers should do a literature search for review question to decrease bias and increase search sensitivity. In ideal situation, you can ask a librarian to help you or monitor your search.

As it was mentioned previously, the main search of the systematic review is a complex method in which we try to find all associated literature. In this step, we need to write a syntax to cover all relevant studies.

A good search strategy should cover most of associated publications.

What is syntax?

Formulating words and phrases in a specific order to find relevant publications is called syntax. The method of syntax writing differs between databases; however, they should support each other. First, we write an exact syntax for each database, and then customize it. This customizing is based on the role and language of each database.

Search sources

We need databases and resources for literature search. Therefore, before starting the review search, we must specify the databases that will be used for the systematic search.

Bibliographic databases

Online databases are the primary sources of searching the literature for systematic reviews, and most systematic reviews rely on bibliographic databases as their primary source of search. Several online bibliographic databases include journal articles, books, dissertation, and conference abstracts. Subject headings or subject index are used to index the content of bibliographic databases.

Most databases provide the opportunity to export all retrieved results into bibliographic software (such as Endnote) to save time and effort.

MEDLINE

MEDLINE is an electronic bibliographic database of the national library of Medicine of the United States, which includes over 40 million (until 2022) records in the field of biomedicine. More than 5200 journals in 40 different languages are indexed in MEDLINE. It includes literature from 1966 to the present, and some previous publications [1].

PubMed can freely access MEDLINE. Also, other database vendors including, Ovid, ProQuest, and EBSCO provide access to MEDLINE, however an institutional subscription is needed (Fig. 5.1).

MeSH (Medical Subject Headings) is the thesaurus of PubMed, used for indexing articles. It allows researchers to retrieve information even when using various terms by other researchers referring the same topic.

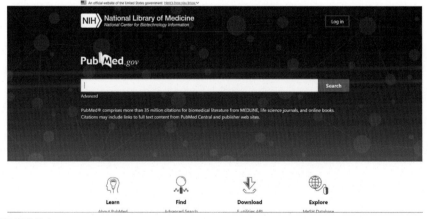

FIGURE 5.1

Preface of PubMed.

Embase

Embase (Excerpta Medica Database) is a European database, including more than 22 million records and 7600 journals over 95 countries since 1947. Emtree is the Embase thesaurus, consisting of index terms, which are organized in a tree structure [2]. More than half of the journals that are indexed in Embase are published in European countries.

Elsevier, ProQuest, or Ovid subscription access Embase. It is reported that Embase approximately covers most indexed records in MEDLINE (Fig. 5.2).

Scopus

Scopus is another bibliographic database of abstracts and citations that is published by Elsevier since 2004, including more than 3500 journals of different fields as well as biomedicine, social science, physics, etc. It can be accessed through Elsevier, and covers more than 40 languages [3] (Fig. 5.3).

Web of Science

Web of Science, also known as Web of Knowledge, is a comprehensive literature database including different disciplines such as science, social science, humanities, arts, etc. Six indexing databases are included in Web of science: Science Citation Index Expanded; Social Sciences Citation Index; Arts & Humanities Citation Index; Emerging Sources Citation Index; Book Citation Index. Web of science is published

FIGURE 5.2

Preface of embase.

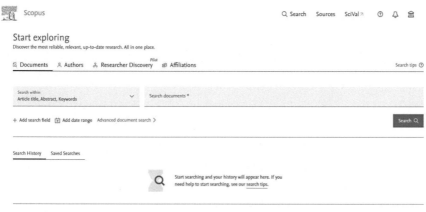

FIGURE 5.3

Preface of scopus.

by Clarivate since 1900, including 79 million core collections, and 171 million platforms. It can be accessed by institutional subscription through Clavirate (Fig. 5.4) [4].

It should be noted that based on our topic, we may need to search other databases such as PsycINFO (psychology), and Allied and Complementary Medicine Database, AMED (alternative therapy). Therefore, along with four main databases, subject-specific databases can also be searched.

After obtaining the results of each database, please record the number of retrieved studies from each database in a sheet to report in the results part of the manuscript.

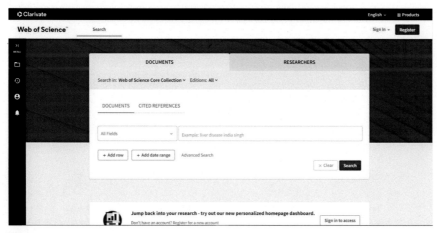

FIGURE 5.4

Preface of web of science.

Grey literature

There are some other literatures that aren't indexed in online databases, which are called gray literature, including dissertations and theses, conference abstracts, references of included articles (particularly review ones), registered trials, newsletters, Patents, etc.

MeSH terms in PubMed

The **first step** of writing a good syntax is finding, and selecting associated words of your subject. For example, if you want to plan a systematic review and meta-analysis regarding bladder dysfunction, you have to find all terms that are related to bladder dysfunction. So, we can search MeSH database to find these words (Figs. 5.5—5.7).

Follow these steps to find a collection of associated words:

PubMed > MeSH database > search a word in the query.

For "bladder dysfunction" these MeSH terms have been suggested:

- Neurogenic Urinary Bladder
- Bladder, Neurogenic

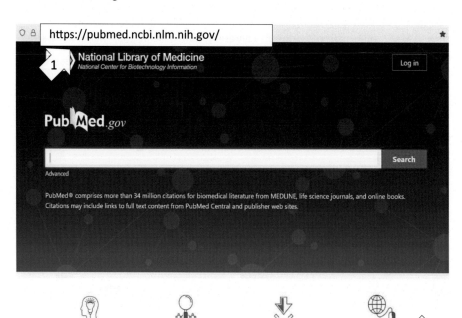

FIGURE 5.5

MeSH database.

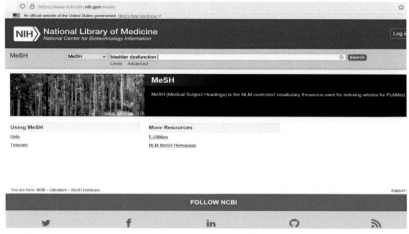

FIGURE 5.6

Searching keyword in the MeSH database.

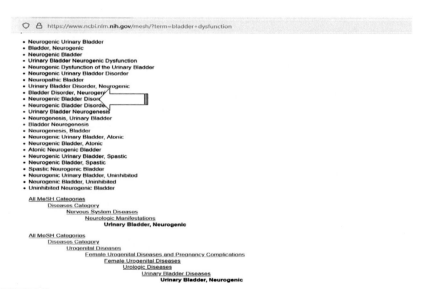

FIGURE 5.7

Associated words are listed.

- Neurogenic Bladder
- Urinary Bladder Neurogenic Dysfunction
- Neurogenic Dysfunction of the Urinary Bladder
- Neurogenic Urinary Bladder Disorder
- Neuropathic Bladder

- Urinary Bladder Disorder, Neurogenic
- Bladder Disorder, Neurogenic
- Neurogenic Bladder Disorders
- Neurogenic Bladder Disorder
- Urinary Bladder Neurogenesis
- Neurogenesis, Urinary Bladder
- Bladder Neurogenesis
- Neurogenesis, Bladder
- Neurogenic Urinary Bladder, Atonic
- Neurogenic Bladder, Atonic
- Atonic Neurogenic Bladder
- Neurogenic Urinary Bladder, Spastic
- Neurogenic Bladder, Spastic
- Spastic Neurogenic Bladder
- Neurogenic Urinary Bladder, Uninhibited
- Neurogenic Bladder, Uninhibited
- Uninhibited Neurogenic Bladder

Emtree:

Emtree is the thesaurus of unique subheadings in Embase that is used to find relevant keywords for search strategy. For each subheading, Emtree provides the number of unique results in the database, synonyms, and the definition in Dorland's dictionary. Emtree can be reached following these steps (Fig. 5.8):

Embase > Emtree > search a word in query

FIGURE 5.8

Searching keyword in emtree database.

Exact phrases

As a **second step**, We need to know the search terminology to write a good syntax. An exact phrase is a collection of words that are usually used together.

They can include two or more words:

Example: "**breast cancer**" will yield results that contain the exact phrase breast cancer. Without the quotation marks, you will get results that include these terms separately (the database would search breast AND cancer).

Other examples: "multiple sclerosis", "Vitamin D", "Neuromyelitis Optica Spectrum Disorder", "Bladder Dysfunction".

Tags

When you search the dictionary for the word "Tag" you find: "*a label attached to someone or something for identification or to give other information*". Also, in writing a syntax, we use tags to help the databases to identify the words we desire in the text. For example, if we want to find all the publications that "multiple sclerosis" in their titles, we can search: "multiple sclerosis"[ti].

This tag means: find any publications that have been mentioned "multiple sclerosis" in their title.

The critical point is that each database has its' monopolized tags, therefore they are mostly the same. Now, we are going to learn more tags in different databases.

PubMed

a. All Fields [all]
b. Title [ti]
c. Title/Abstract [tiab]
d. MeSH Terms [mh]

Notice: User's guide in PubMed.gov is available to find more tags.

Embase

a. ti, ab: Title/Abstract
b. all: all fields

Notice: "Search tips" in this database is available to investigate more tags.

Scopus

a. Abstract (ABS)
b. All Fields (ALL)

   c. Doc Title (TITLE)
   d. Doc Title, Abstract (TITLE-ABS)
   e. Doc Title, Abstract, Keyword (TITLE-ABS-KEY)
   f. Doc Title, Abstract, Keyword, Author (TITLE-ABS-KEY-AUTH)

Notice: Field codes in advanced search are available to find more tags.

If you do not write the tags it means all field (If there is no tag, the default configuration of some databases is to consider the term in all fields). Therefore we suggest always writing them down in your syntax.

Web of Science

a. TS = Topic
b. TI=Title
c. AB = Abstract
d. PY= Published Year
e. ALL = All Fields

Notice: "Field tags" in advanced search is available to find more tags for Web of Science.

Operators

We use the operators to connect words during writing syntax. AND, OR, and NOT are the most frequently used operators.

a. AND:
   We use AND when we want to include publications with all desired words. For example, when we want to find all articles that reported "restless leg syndrome" beside "multiple sclerosis", in all fields,
   we should search: "Multiple Sclerosis" [all] AND "Restless Leg Syndrome" [all].
   It has been suggested to use a collection of words using MeSH database. It has been written like this: *Neurogenesis, Bladder* or *Bladder Disorder, Neurogenic*. We need to use AND to connect these collections.
   In this example, we should write like this: (*Neurogenesis AND Bladder*) or ("*Bladder Disorder" AND "Neurogenic"*)
   parenthesis shows that they are a collection of words, and we used the "" to define the exact phrases.

b. OR:
   It is used to connect synonyms of a keyword. For example, for bladder dysfunction we write as follow:
   " Neurogenic Urinary Bladder" **OR** (Bladder AND Neurogenic) **OR** "Neurogenic Bladder" **OR** "Urinary Bladder Neurogenic Dysfunction" **OR** "Neurogenic Dysfunction of the Urinary Bladder" **OR** "Neurogenic Urinary Bladder

Disorder" **OR** "Neuropathic Bladder" **OR** ("Urinary Bladder Disorder" AND Neurogenic) **OR** ("Bladder Disorder" AND Neurogenic) **OR** "Neurogenic Bladder Disorders" **OR** "Neurogenic Bladder Disorder" **OR** "Urinary Bladder Neurogenesis" **OR** (Neurogenesis AND "Urinary Bladder") **OR** "Bladder Neurogenesis" **OR** (Neurogenesis AND Bladder) **OR** ("Neurogenic Urinary Bladder" AND Atonic) **OR** ("Neurogenic Bladder" AND Atonic) **OR** "Atonic Neurogenic Bladder" **OR** ("Neurogenic Urinary Bladder" **OR** Spastic) **OR** ("Neurogenic Bladder" AND Spastic) **OR** "Spastic Neurogenic Bladder" **OR** ("Neurogenic Urinary Bladder" AND Uninhibited) **OR** "Neurogenic Bladder" AND Uninhibited) **OR** "Uninhibited Neurogenic Bladder"

When we use "OR" as an operator, the order of the words is not important.

c. NOT:

It is not a useful operator in syntax writing for systematic reviews. For example, when we write a syntax such as "multiple sclerosis" AND NOT mice, it means that we search for the articles that include "multiple sclerosis" but they do not include mice.

PubMed syntax
Inclusive search strategy for PubMed

The inclusive search is the search with the highest coverage of related publications. An inclusive search usually includes several unrelated articles, which prolongs your screening project. Now, we go through the example.

We are going to write a search syntax for this title: prevalence of restless leg syndrome in multiple sclerosis patients.

For this aim we should choose two keywords, which are "restless leg syndrome" and "Multiple Sclerosis". Inclusive syntax for PubMed is as follows:

Example 1.1.
((Sclerosis AND multiple) OR (sclerosis AND disseminated) OR "disseminated sclerosis" OR "multiple sclerosis" OR "acute fulminating")
    AND
    ("Restless Leg*" OR "Willis–Ekbom Disease" OR (Disease AND "Willis Ekbom") OR "Wittmaack-Ekbom Syndrome" OR (Syndrome AND "Wittmaack-Ekbom") OR "Willis-Ekbom Disease" OR (Disease AND "Willis-Ekbom") OR "Willis-Ekbom Syndrome" OR (Syndrome AND "Willis-Ekbom") OR "Wittmaack Ekbom Syndrome" OR (Syndrome AND "Wittmaack Ekbom") OR "Restless Leg Syndrome" OR (Syndrome AND "Restless Leg") OR "Willis Ekbom Syndrome" OR (Syndrome AND "Willis Ekbom"))

In another example, we are going to write an inclusive syntax for a study that has been conducted to evaluate the prevalence of urinary dysfunction in patients with Neuromyelitis Optica spectrum disorder. The two keywords are:

"urinary dysfunction" and "Neuromyelitis Optica spectrum disorder":

Example 1.2.
("NMO Spectrum Disorder" OR NMOSD OR NMO OR "Devic's Disease" OR "Devic's Syndrome" OR "Neuromyelitis Optica" OR "Neuromyelitis Optica Spectrum Disorder")
    AND
    ("Urinary Bladder" OR (Bladder AND Urinary) OR Bladder OR "Bladder Detrusor Muscle" OR "Bladder Detrusor Muscles" OR ("Detrusor Muscle*" AND Bladder) OR "Detrusor Urinae" OR "Urinary Incontinence" OR (Incontinence AND "UrinaryUrination") OR Micturition "Urinary Incontinence" OR (Incontinence AND Urinary) OR "Urinary Tract*" OR (Tract* AND Urinary) OR ("Urinary Bladder" AND Neurogenic) OR "Neurogenic Urinary Bladder" OR (Bladder AND Neurogenic) OR "Neurogenic Bladder" OR "Urinary Bladder Neurogenic Dysfunction" OR "Neurogenic Dysfunction of the Urinary Bladder" OR "Neurogenic Urinary Bladder Disorder" OR "Neuropathic Bladder" OR ("Urinary Bladder Disorder" AND Neurogenic) OR ("Bladder Disorder" AND Neurogenic) OR "Neurogenic Bladder Disorder" OR "Urinary Bladder Neurogenesis" OR (Neurogenesis AND "Urinary Bladder") OR "Bladder Neurogenesis" OR (Neurogenesis AND Bladder) OR ("Neurogenic Urinary Bladder" AND Atonic) OR ("Neurogenic Bladder" AND Atonic) OR "Atonic Neurogenic Bladder" OR ("Neurogenic Urinary Bladder" AND Spastic) OR ("Neurogenic Bladder" AND Spastic) OR "Spastic Neurogenic Bladder" OR ("Neurogenic Urinary Bladder" AND Uninhibited) OR ("Neurogenic Bladder" AND Uninhibited) OR "Uninhibited Neurogenic Bladder" OR Incontinence OR Micturition OR Overactive OR Underactive OR "postvoid residual" OR retention).

Embase search strategy

We are going to write our syntax in Embase. The inclusive syntax for prevalence of restless leg syndrome in patients with multiple sclerosis in Embase is as follow:

Example 1.3.
((Sclerosis AND multiple) OR (sclerosis AND disseminated) OR 'disseminated sclerosis' OR 'multiple sclerosis' OR 'acute fulminating')
    AND
    ('Restless Leg*' OR 'Willis Ekbom Disease' OR (Disease AND 'Willis Ekbom') OR 'Wittmaack-Ekbom Syndrome' OR (Syndrome AND 'Wittmaack-Ekbom') OR 'Willis-Ekbom Disease' OR (Disease AND 'Willis-Ekbom') OR 'Willis-Ekbom Syndrome' OR (Syndrome AND 'Willis-Ekbom') OR 'Wittmaack Ekbom Syndrome' OR (Syndrome AND 'Wittmaack Ekbom') OR 'Restless Leg Syndrome' OR (Syndrome AND 'Restless Leg') OR 'Willis Ekbom Syndrome' OR (Syndrome AND 'Willis Ekbom')))

The excusive syntax for Embase is:

Example 1.4.
((Sclerosis:ti,ab AND multiple:ti,ab) OR (sclerosis:ti,ab AND disseminated:ti,ab) OR 'disseminated sclerosis':ti,ab OR 'multiple sclerosis':ti,ab OR 'acute fulminating':ti,ab).
    AND
    ('Restless Leg*':ti,ab OR 'Willis Ekbom Disease':ti,ab OR (Disease:ti,ab AND 'Willis Ekbom': ti,ab) OR 'Wittmaack-Ekbom Syndrome':ti,ab OR (Syndrome:ti,ab AND 'Wittmaack-Ekbom': ti,ab) OR 'Willis-Ekbom Disease':ti,ab OR (Disease:ti,ab AND 'Willis-Ekbom':ti,ab) OR '

—cont'd

Willis-Ekbom Syndrome':ti,ab OR (Syndromc:ti,ab AND 'Willis-Ekbom':ti,ab) OR 'Wittmaack Ekbom Syndrome':ti,ab OR (Syndrome:ti,ab AND 'Wittmaack Ekbom':ti,ab) OR 'Restless Leg Syndrome':ti,ab OR (Syndrome:ti,ab AND 'Restless Leg':ti,ab) OR 'Willis Ekbom Syndrome': ti,ab OR (Syndrome:ti,ab AND 'Willis Ekbom':ti,ab))

Scopus search strategy

Customizing the syntax of Restless leg syndrome and Multiple Sclerosis in inclusive strategy:

Example 1.5.
((ALL(Sclerosis) AND ALL(multiple)) OR (ALL(sclerosis) AND ALL(disseminated)) OR ALL("disseminated sclerosis") OR ALL("multiple sclerosis") OR ALL("acute fulminating"))
 AND
 (ALL("Restless Leg*") OR ALL("Willis Ekbom Disease") OR (ALL(Disease) AND ALL("Willis Ekbom")) OR ALL("Wittmaack-Ekbom Syndrome") OR (ALL(Syndrome) AND ALL("Wittmaack-Ekbom")) OR ALL("Willis-Ekbom Disease") OR (ALL(Disease) AND ALL("Willis-Ekbom")) OR ALL("Willis-Ekbom Syndrome") OR (ALL(Syndrome) AND ALL("Willis-Ekbom")) OR ALL("Wittmaack Ekbom Syndrome") OR (ALL(Syndrome) AND ALL("Wittmaack Ekbom")) OR ALL("Restless Leg Syndrome") OR (ALL(Syndrome) AND ALL("Restless Leg")) OR ALL("Willis Ekbom Syndrome") OR (ALL(Syndrome) AND ALL("-Willis Ekbom")))

Exclusive syntax for "restless leg syndrome" AND "multiple sclerosis" in Scopus.

Example 1.6.
((TITLE-ABS(Sclerosis) AND TITLE-ABS (multiple)) OR (TITLE-ABS(sclerosis) AND TITLE-ABS(disseminated)) OR TITLE-ABS("disseminated sclerosis") OR TITLE-ABS("multiple sclerosis") OR TITLE-ABS("acute fulminating"))
 AND
 (TITLE-ABS("Restless Leg*") OR TITLE-ABS("Willis Ekbom Disease") OR (TITLE-ABS(Disease) AND TITLE-ABS("Willis Ekbom")) OR TITLE-ABS("Wittmaack-Ekbom Syndrome") OR (TITLE-ABS(Syndrome) AND TITLE-ABS("Wittmaack-Ekbom")) OR TITLE-ABS("Willis-Ekbom Disease") OR (TITLE-ABS(Disease) AND TITLE-ABS("Willis-Ekbom")) OR TITLE-ABS("Willis-Ekbom Syndrome") OR (TITLE-ABS(Syndrome) AND TITLE-ABS("Willis-Ekbom")) OR TITLE-ABS("Wittmaack Ekbom Syndrome") OR (TITLE-ABS(Syndrome) AND TITLE-ABS("Wittmaack Ekbom")) OR TITLE-ABS("Restless Leg Syndrome") OR (TITLE-ABS(Syndrome) AND TITLE-ABS("Restless Leg")) OR TITLE-ABS("Willis Ekbom Syndrome") OR (TITLE-ABS(Syndrome) AND TITLE-ABS("Willis Ekbom"))) (Fig. 5.9).

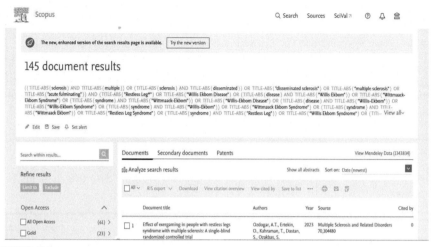

FIGURE 5.9

Scopus search result.

Web of science strategy

Inclusive syntax of restless leg syndrome and Multiple sclerosis in Web of Science database is as follows:

Example 1.7.
((ALL=(Sclerosis) AND ALL=(multiple)) OR (ALL=(sclerosis) AND ALL=(disseminated)) OR ALL=("disseminated sclerosis") OR ALL=("multiple sclerosis") OR ALL=("acute fulminating"))
    AND
    (ALL=("Restless Leg*") OR ALL=("Willis Ekbom Disease") OR (ALL=(Disease) AND ALL=("Willis Ekbom")) OR ALL=("Wittmaack-Ekbom Syndrome") OR (ALL=(Syndrome) AND ALL=("Wittmaack-Ekbom")) OR ALL=("Willis-Ekbom Disease") OR (ALL=(Disease) AND ALL=("Willis-Ekbom")) OR ALL=("Willis-Ekbom Syndrome") OR (ALL=(Syndrome) AND ALL=("Willis-Ekbom")) OR ALL=("Wittmaack Ekbom Syndrome") OR (ALL=(Syndrome) AND ALL=("Wittmaack Ekbom")) OR ALL=("Restless Leg Syndrome") OR (ALL=(Syndrome) AND ALL=("Restless Leg")) OR ALL=("Willis Ekbom Syndrome") OR (ALL=(Syndrome) AND ALL=("Willis Ekbom")))

The **excusive syntax** for Web of Science is as follow:

Example 1.8.
((TS=(Sclerosis) AND TS=(multiple)) OR (TS=(sclerosis) AND TS=(disseminated)) OR TS=("disseminated sclerosis") OR TS=("multiple sclerosis") OR TS=("acute fulminating"))
    AND
    (TS=("Restless Leg*") OR TS=("Willis Ekbom Disease") OR (TS=(Disease) AND TS=("Willis Ekbom")) OR TS=("Wittmaack-Ekbom Syndrome") OR (TS=(Syndrome) AND TS=("Witt-maack-Ekbom")) OR TS=("Willis-Ekbom Disease") OR (TS=(Disease) AND TS=("Willis-Ekbom")) OR TS=("Willis-Ekbom Syndrome") OR (TS=(Syndrome) AND TS=("Willis-Ekbom")) OR TS=("Wittmaack Ekbom Syndrome") OR (TS=(Syndrome) AND TS=("Wittmaack Ekbom")))

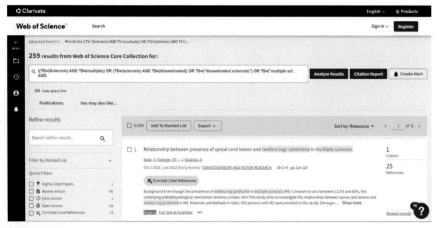

FIGURE 5.10

Web of Science search result.

—cont'd

OR TS=("Restless Leg Syndrome") OR (TS=(Syndrome) AND TS=("Restless Leg")) OR TS=("Willis Ekbom Syndrome") OR (TS=(Syndrome) AND TS=("Willis Ekbom"))) (Fig. 5.10).

Summary

In this chapter, an overview of systematic search and practical examples in four main online bibliographic databases were provided. Also, some other principal points in search were discussed, which may help to develop a better and comprehensive systematic review.

References

[1] https://www.nlm.nih.gov/medline/medline_overview.html.
[2] https://www.sciencedirect.com/topics/immunology-and-microbiology/embase.
[3] https://en.wikipedia.org/wiki/Scopus.
[4] https://en.wikipedia.org/wiki/Web_of_Science#Coverage.

Search record screening

6

Mohsen Rastkar

Tehran University of Medical Sciences, Tehran, Iran

Introduction

The most important step after systematic search is screening of retrieved results. Based on the inclusion and exclusion criteria, the search records should be carefully evaluated in order to determine their eligibility for inclusion in the systematic review. In this chapter, we will go through the screening phase of systematic review journey [1].

Exporting search results

After conducting the systematic search in the predefined databases, the search results should be merged. Then team members could start screening the search results and selecting relevant results. The process of exporting the results from the four discussed databases can be done as discussed below:

PubMed

In the PubMed database, the results can be exported by "Send to" option, which gives four choices of "Clipboard," "My Bibliography," "Collections," and "citation manager" (for easy access and using records in Citation Manager, the last option is desirable) (Fig. 6.1).

Embase

In Embase database, you can download the search results using the "export" option and choosing output file format (Fig. 6.2).

Scopus

Like the previous databases, in Scopus, the search results can be downloaded using the "export" option after choosing search records and format of the output file (Fig. 6.3).

Systematic Review and Meta-Analysis. https://doi.org/10.1016/B978-0-443-13428-9.00006-9

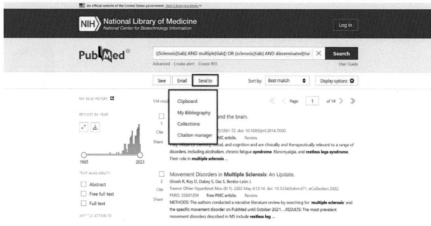

FIGURE 6.1

Downloading results from PubMed.

FIGURE 6.2

Downloading results from Embase.

Also, in Scopus, you can select which information of each record you desire to be downloaded including citation information, bibliographical information, abstract and keywords, funding details, and other information (Fig. 6.4).

Web of Science

Web of Science database gives you the option of downloading the search records in different output formats such as compatible formats for Endnote online, Endnote desktop, Excel, BibTeX, etc (Fig. 6.5).

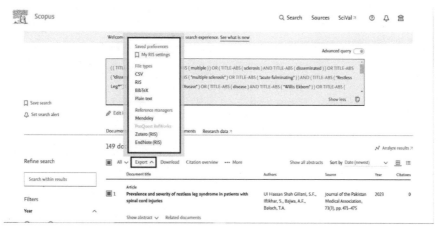

FIGURE 6.3

Downloading results from Scopus.

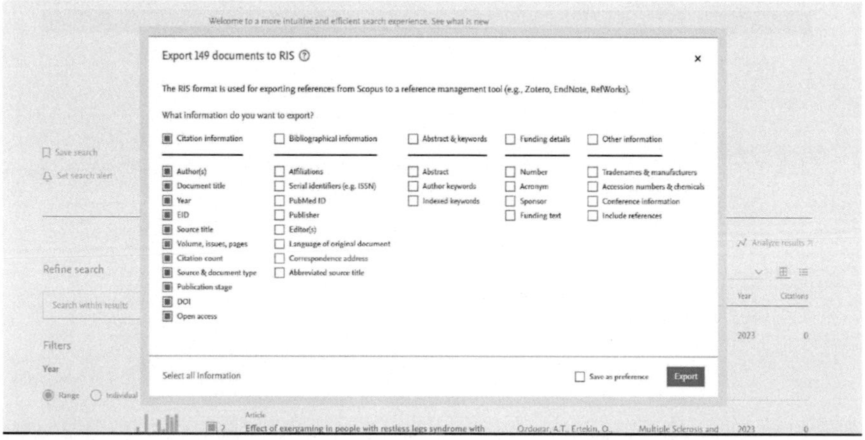

FIGURE 6.4

Selecting citation information in Scopus.

Merging search records

After downloading the search results from all databases, you can use various softwares to merge the records such as Mendeley and Endnote.

Endnote is one of the most widely used reference manager software, which can be used to save and manage search records. Fig. 6.6 shows a sample library of Endnote.

Since the results of different databases may overlap, there will be duplicate records in your library. Before applying inclusion and exclusion criteria to your list of studies, you have to omit duplicate records in your library.

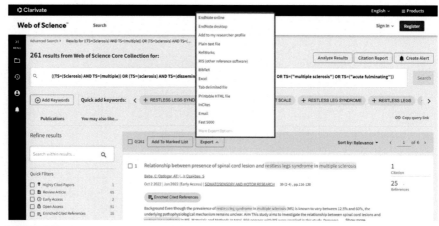

FIGURE 6.5

Downloading citations in Web of Science.

FIGURE 6.6

Sample library of Endnote.

In the Endnote, you can find and delete duplicates by "find duplicates" option in the "Library" tab. However, this feature may not cover all duplicates, so the records should be checked manually to ensure that there are no more duplicates.

Screening process

Screening of retrieved records could be done in two sections [2]:

(1) Title/Abstract screening: In this stage, the titles and abstracts of records should be screened based on the inclusion and exclusion criteria.

In this stage, it is better to have two independent researchers to screen titles and abstracts to have a robust screening phase.

(2) Full-text screening: In this phase, potentially eligible records will be evaluated based on their full-text.

After screening titles and abstracts, you have to obtain the full texts of marked records for further assessment.

In this step, you should have the full text of the potential references (either printed or electronic version) and also your inclusion and exclusion criteria next to each other. At least two researchers should evaluate the full texts to increase the accuracy of the screening phase. If there are any conflicts between two reviewers, they can resolve this issue by asking a third party.

If you have no access to the full text of an eligible record (even through your institutional library), you can email the corresponding author and ask for full text of the record. Sometimes authors make their records freely available through some social media.

After carefully evaluation of each record, you should decide if the record is included in the systematic review or not. If not, you should write the exclusion reason.

Screening softwares

There are softwares which can help you through screening process [3]:

1. EPPI-Reviewer 4,
2. Covidence,
3. DistillerSR,
4. System for the Unified Management, Assessment, and Review of Information (SUMARI),
5. Rayyan QCRI
6. Sysrev.

Only Rayyan QCRI is free, and we will show an example in this software (Fig. 6.7) [4]. It is a web and also mobile app that helps screening of retrieved records.

To create new review in Rayyan, you should enter the title, research field, review type, and review domain (Fig. 6.8).

Then, you can upload your reference manager file such as Endnote file (upload the file where the flash is) (Fig. 6.9).

Then you can open each reference and evaluate the title, and the abstract (Fig. 6.10).

FIGURE 6.7

Preface of Rayyan QCRI.

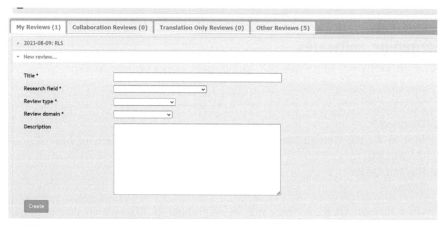

FIGURE 6.8

Creating new review.

New search for Review: RLS

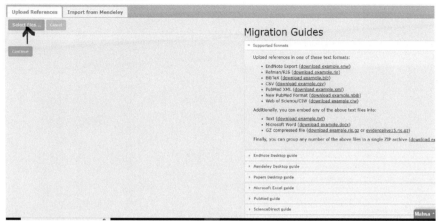

FIGURE 6.9

Uploading reference.

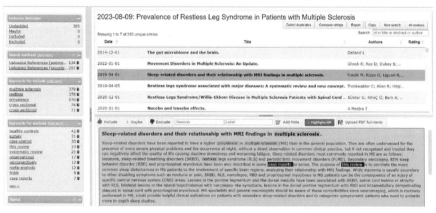

FIGURE 6.10

Review main page.

References

[1] Dissemination C. Systematic reviews: CRD's guidance for undertaking reviews in healthcare. York: University of York NHS Centre for Reviews & Dissemination; 2009.

[2] Higgins J, Deeks J. Selecting studies and collecting data. Version 5.1. 0 (updated March 2011). In: Higgins JPT, Green S, editors. Cochrane handbook for systematic reviews of interventions. The Cochrane Collaboration; 2011. Available from: handbook cochrane org. 2011.

[3] https://ktdrr.org/resources/sr-resources/tools.html.

[4] https://www.rayyan.ai/.

Data extraction

Narges Ebrahimi[1,2,3]

[1]*Department of Immunology, Faculty of Medicine, Isfahan University of Medical Sciences, Isfahan, Iran;* [2]*Immunodeficiency Diseases Research Center, Isfahan University of Medical Sciences, Isfahan, Iran;* [3]*Isfahan Neurosciences Research Center, Isfahan University of Medical Sciences, Isfahan, Iran*

Introduction

Data extraction is an important step in conducting a systematic review and meta-analysis. Accurate and precise data extraction is essential to ensure the validity and reliability of the results.

It would be ideal for two independent researchers to do data extraction to confirm the validity of the obtained data.

This chapter provides a step-by-step guide for the data extraction process of systematic reviews.

Step 1: Develop a data extraction form

The first step in extracting data is to develop a data extraction form that includes all required information. The form should be designed to ensure that all necessary data are extracted systematically and consistently across all included studies. The data extraction form should include information on study characteristics, population characteristics, intervention details, outcome measures, and any other relevant variables.

To develop a data extraction form, you should:

1. **Define the data you need:** The first step is to define your research question and the specific data you need to answer. This will help you determine what data to extract and what variables to include in the form.

   (Defining the review question is explained in detail in Chapter 4).

1. **Build a template for the form:** Use a spreadsheet, such as an Excel sheet, to create a template for the data extraction form. Assign a column to each variable.

2. **Define the variables, units, and desired statistical measures:** Define each variable included in the form and its desired measures. For example, if you are

Systematic Review and Meta-Analysis. https://doi.org/10.1016/B978-0-443-13428-9.00007-0

collecting data regarding the weight of newborns, you should specify whether you will record data as kg or grams. You should also determine if you want data presented as mean or median.

3. **Pilot your form:** Before using the form for extracting data from all included studies, extract data from one or two studies and enter the form to see if it works.
4. **Revise the form:** Based on the feedback you get from the pilot phase, revise the form to improve the data collection process.

Step 2: Collaborative oversight

1. **Train people who are going to extract data:** If multiple individuals will be extracting data from the included studies, provide them with **clear** instructions on **how** to use the form and **what** data to collect.
2. **Monitor data extraction:** Monitor the data extraction process to ensure that data has been collected accurately and consistently. At least two independent researchers should extract data. If more than one researcher is extracting data, then you can check if both have the same understanding of the variables and data that you need.

   For study characteristics, researchers should record study design, inclusion and exclusion criteria, the number of participants, duration of follow-up (if applicable), intervention method or performance protocol, diagnostic protocol, instrument and questionnaire used in the study as well as primary and secondary outcomes. It is essential to ensure that these characteristics are consistently recorded for all studies to maintain uniformity in the data extraction process.

$$Prevalence\ of\ RLS\ among\ MS\ patients = \frac{Total\ number\ of\ MS\ with\ RLS}{Total\ number\ of\ MS\ Patients}$$

   Here is an example of what a data extraction form might look like for a study on patient outcomes (Table 7.1)

   For the example where we estimate the pooled prevalence of restless leg syndrome (RLS) in patients with multiple sclerosis (MS), we need the total number of patients with MS and the number of patients suffering from RLS in each included study.

   The following form is a sample of the data extraction form, which is derived from our recently published manuscript (the prevalence of RLS in patients with MS: a systematic review and meta-analysis—an update) (Table 7.2).
3. **Select appropriate software or tools:** Besides paper-based data extraction forms, you can custom proper software to do data extraction.

   Several software programs are available for data extraction, such as EPPI-Reviewer, Covidence, and DistillerSR. These software can streamline the data extraction process and facilitate the management of extracted data. Researchers could import and export data, conduct duplicate extraction, and record quality control checks.

Table 7.1 Example of data extraction form

Variable	Description
Study ID	A unique identifier for each study included in the review.
First Author(s) name	List the primary authors of the study for citation and reference purposes.
Year of Publication	The year the study was published, which can help contextualize the findings within a temporal framework.
Study Design	Type of study (e.g., randomized controlled trial, cohort study, case-control, cross-sectional).
Inclusion Criteria	Specific criteria for including studies in the review (e.g., participant characteristics, interventions).
Exclusion Criteria	Criteria employed to exclude studies, which helps clarify the boundaries of the review.
Sample Size	Total number of participants in each study, including any specific subgroup sizes if applicable. (e.g., case and control or placebo and intervention group)
Participant Characteristics	Key demographic details, such as age, sex, ethnicity, health status of participants like comorbidities and current treatments, family history, addiction or habits (if applicable and associate to results)
Follow-Up Duration	Length of time participants were followed post-intervention or during data collection.
Intervention Details	Description of the intervention(s), including type, dosage, frequency, and administration method.
Control Group	Information about the control or comparison group, including the nature of the control (e.g., placebo).
Outcome Measures	Primary and secondary outcomes measured, detailing what was assessed, how and what was the unit. (e.g., Count of WBC with CBC test with the unit 10^9/L; e.g., Depression score with a valid method and without any special unit (however, it can be yes/no or score etc.)
Measurement Instruments	Tools or questionnaires used to measure outcomes, including their validity and reliability. (e.g., Flow Cytometry or Mass spectrometry etc.; e.g., BDI Questionnaire, PET scan, Psychologist diagnosis) "Please note that some articles consider clinician diagnoses (based on established criteria) as valid methods. However, patient self-reports, even if supported by a specialist's opinion, are not sufficiently reliable."
Results	Key findings related to the primary and secondary outcomes, including mean (SD), effect sizes[a] and confidence intervals.
Mortality status Safety and/or efficacy	This characters are completely related to your design, out comes (primary and secondary) and the subject (e.g., Group A reported 9.5 (out of 100,000) however the other group, B, has been reported 3 out of 100,000; e.g., Safety: Hospitalization rates associated with the intervention or treatment.) Efficacy: Reduction in disability scores measured over the study period.

Continued

Table 7.1 Example of data extraction form—*cont'd*

Variable	Description
Statistical Analysis	The statistical methods used in the study, including any adjustments for confounding factors.
Limitations	Noted limitations acknowledged by the authors that may affect the interpretation of the results.
Notes on Study Quality	An assessment of the methodological quality or risk of bias in the study, using a standardized tool if applicable (Refer to Chapter 8 for more information).

BDI, *Beck's depression inventory;* PET, *positron emission tomography.*
[a] *Effect size is a way to measure the strength of the statistical relationship between two variables. It is a standardized measure that is used to indicate the magnitude of the effect of an intervention or treatment. In other words, how big the effect is and logically unitless.*

After entering your username and password in EPPI Reviewer, you can create your review by hitting create review button.

Then, you will choose the name and enter. You will see the page below, which allows you to import your records and manage duplicates.

Step 3: Data extraction by two independent reviewers and quality checks

Two independent reviewers should extract data to ensure the accuracy and consistency of extracted data.

Quality checks should be performed periodically throughout the data extraction process to guarantee that data are extracted accurately and consistently. They could ask a third one to solve the problem if any discrepancies remain.

Step 4: Document the data extraction process

It is crucial to document the data extraction method to warrant the transparency of the process and allow readers to evaluate the quality of the review process. Authors should keep detailed records of the data extraction process, including the search strategy, applied soft-wares or tools, the number of screened studies, the number of studies finally included, and the reasons for excluding studies.

Table 7.2 Sample of data extraction.

First author name	Publication year	Country of origin	Diagnostic criteria	Total MS female/male	Mean (SD) age	Mean (SD) EDSS	Total RLS.MS
Tobias Monschein	2021	Austria	IRLSSG	1,177,938	36.3(9.6)		28RR: 22SP: 2 PP: 4
H.A. Hensen	2020	Australia	NR	1,118,526	NR		29
Bouhlal, M	2020	Netherlands	IRLSSG	805,327	NR		27
Katie L.J	2020	Brazil	IRLSSG	27,522,352	59.7 (10.1)		74RR: 48SP: 17 PP: 9
Meral Seferoğlu	2020	Turkey	IRLSSG	46	41.07(7.74)		19
M. Manconia	2007	Italy	Clinical interview	15,610,056	40.7 (10.4)		51RR: 35SP: 7 PP: 9

ABS, Congress Abstract; F.RLS.MS, Female MS patients with RLS; IRLSSG, International Restless Legs Syndrome Study Group; M.RLS.MS, Male MS patients with RLS; PP, Primary Progressive MS; RR, Relapsing-Remitting MS; SP, Secondary Progressive MS.

Data presented were extracted from: Zali A, et al. The prevalence of restless legs syndrome (RLS) in patients with multiple sclerosis (MS): a systematic review and meta-analysis—an update. Neurol Sci Off J Italian Neurol Soc Italian Soc Clin Neurophys 2023;44(1):67–82. https://doi.org/10.1007/s10072-022-06364-6

Conclusion

Data extraction is a critical step in the systematic review and meta-analysis process, and authors must ensure that the process is systematic, transparent, and replicable. Developing a comprehensive data extraction form, selecting appropriate software, conducting double extraction, and quality checks, documenting the data extraction process, and reporting the data extraction process precisely is essential for conducting high-quality systematic reviews.

Assessment of risk of bias in included studies

8

Narges Ebrahimi[1,2,3]

[1]*Immunodeficiency Diseases Research Center, Isfahan University of Medical Sciences, Isfahan, Iran;* [2]*Department of Immunology, Faculty of Medicine, Isfahan University of Medical Sciences, Isfahan, Iran;* [3]*Isfahan Neurosciences Research Center, Isfahan University of Medical Sciences, Isfahan, Iran*

Types of quality assessment tools
Introduction

To ensure that systematic reviews and meta-analyses are free of bias, it is necessary to use appropriate quality assessment tools to evaluate included studies.

Different tools are developed for different types of studies. In this chapter, we will discuss the different types of quality assessment tools that can be used in systematic reviews and meta-analyses.

Jadad scale

The questions and guidance of this questionnaire have been described as follows:

The Jadad scale is widely used for quality assessment of randomized controlled trials (RCTs). It was developed by Jadad et al. in 1996 and included five questions regarding three topics: randomization, blinding, and withdrawals/dropouts. Each question could be scored between 0 and 1, with a possible score of 5. Studies with scores 3 and 5 are considered high quality.

The Jadad scale is easy to use and has good interrater reliability.

The questions are as below:

1. Was the study described as randomized?
   Answer: Yes/No.
   Evaluate whether the study clearly states that it was randomized. If the study is described as randomized, please consider the randomization method. Sometimes, it is confusing as the method is considered a randomized study but lacks true randomization.
2. Was the method used to generate the sequence of randomization described and appropriate?
   Answer: Yes/No.

Systematic Review and Meta-Analysis. https://doi.org/10.1016/B978-0-443-13428-9.00008-2

Assess whether the study provides a clear description of the method, which was used to generate the randomization sequence. Look for details on methods such as computer-generated random numbers or randomization tables. An appropriate approach ensures that the randomization process is unbiased.

3. Was the study described as double-blind?

Answer: Yes/No.

Determine whether the study explicitly states that it was conducted as a double-blind trial. Double-blinding helps minimize bias by preventing both the participants and the investigators from knowing the treatment assignments.

4. Was the method of double-blinding described and appropriate?

Answer: Yes/No.

Evaluate whether the study provides a clear description of the method, which was used for double-blinding. Look for details on how participants and investigators were blinded to treatment assignments, such as the use of identical placebos. An appropriate method of double-blinding ensures that treatment group assignments do not influence the outcomes.

5. Was there a description of withdrawals and dropouts?

Answer: Yes/No.

Assess whether the study provides detail of withdrawals and dropouts. Look for information on the number of participants who discontinued the study or were lost to follow-up, along with reasons for their withdrawal. Describing withdrawals and dropouts helps assess the potential bias.

Remember to assign a score of 1 for "Yes" and 0 for "No" for each question. The maximum score achievable on the JADAD scale is 5, with higher scores indicating higher methodological quality.

Cochrane Risk of Bias Tool

The Cochrane Risk of Bias tool is comprehensive for the quality assessment of randomized and nonrandomized studies. It comprises six domains related to selection bias, performance bias, detection bias, attrition bias, reporting bias, and other biases(2). Each domain is scored as low risk, high risk, or unclear risk, based on the information provided in the study. The overall risk of bias is then assessed as low, high, or unclear.

The Cochrane Risk of Bias tool is widely used in systematic reviews and meta-analyses and has good interrater reliability. However, it may be time-consuming to apply and requires a detailed understanding of the study design.

1. Random sequence generation:

Answer: Low risk of bias/high risk of bias/unclear risk of bias.

Assess whether the study describes an appropriate method of random sequence generation, such as computer-generated random numbers or randomization tables. A low risk of bias indicates a proper randomization process, while a high risk suggests inadequate randomization methods, increasing the risk of biased group allocation. Unclear risk of bias occurs when the study does not provide sufficient information to judge the random sequence generation process.

2. Allocation concealment:

   Answer: Low risk of bias/high risk of bias/unclear risk of bias.

   Evaluate whether the study describes an appropriate method of allocation concealment, such as central randomization or sequentially numbered, opaque, sealed envelopes. A low risk of bias indicates adequate allocation concealment, while a high risk of bias suggests inadequate methods that may allow for systematic differences in assigning participants to groups. Unclear risk of bias occurs when the study does not provide sufficient information to judge the allocation concealment process.

3. Blinding of participants and personnel:

   Answer: Low risk of bias/high risk of bias/unclear risk of bias.

   Guidance and advice: Determine whether the study describes efforts to blind participants and personnel to the assigned interventions. A low risk of bias indicates successful blinding, reducing performance bias. A high risk of bias suggests that participants or personnel were aware of the assigned interventions, potentially influencing outcomes. Unclear risk of bias occurs when the study does not provide sufficient information to judge the blinding process.

4. Blinding of outcome assessment:

   Answer: Low risk of bias/high risk of bias/unclear risk of bias.

   Assess whether the study describes efforts to blind outcome assessors or not. Low risk of bias indicates successful blinding of outcome assessors and reducing detection bias. A high risk of bias suggests that outcome assessors were aware of the assigned interventions, potentially influencing outcome assessments. An unclear risk of bias occurs when the study does not provide sufficient information to judge the blinding of outcome assessors.

5. Incomplete outcome data:

   Answer: Low risk of bias/high risk of bias/unclear risk of bias.

   Evaluate whether the study adequately addresses missing data and withdrawals/dropouts. A low risk of bias occurs when missing data are minimal and handled appropriately, minimizing attrition bias. A high risk of bias suggests substantial missing data or inadequate handling, potentially introducing bias. An unclear risk of bias occurs when the study does not provide sufficient information to judge the handling of incomplete outcome data.

6. Selective reporting:

   Answer: Low risk of bias/high risk of bias/unclear risk of bias.

   Assess whether the study's reported outcomes match the prespecified or expected outcomes. A low risk of bias indicates complete reporting of all relevant outcomes. A high risk of bias suggests selective reporting of outcomes, potentially distorting the interpretation of study findings. An unclear risk of bias occurs when the study does not provide sufficient information to judge outcomes reporting.

Remember to assign a risk of bias rating for each domain, considering the specific information provided in the study. It is important to consider the risk of bias in each domain to accurately evaluate the study's validity and potential sources of bias.

Please note that the Cochrane Risk of Bias Tool contains additional domains for certain study designs, such as "Baseline characteristics" and "Other biases." The provided guidance focuses on the common domains applicable to most study designs, but it is essential to adapt the assessment based on the specific study design being evaluated.

Risk of bias assessment using the ROBINS-I tool

In the context of systematic reviews and meta-analyses, assessing the risk of bias in included studies is crucial for ensuring the validity and reliability of the conclusions drawn. The Risk Of Bias In Non-randomized Studies of Interventions (ROBINS-I) tool is designed to assess the risk of bias in non-randomized intervention studies, particularly those comparing interventions (observational studies of intervention effects). This tool is essential for identifying potential biases that may arise from study design, implementation, and reporting, which can ultimately affect the outcomes measured and the conclusions drawn. This section provides a comprehensive overview of the ROBINS-I tool, detailing its domains, the questions it poses, and the criteria for rating the risk of bias.

Overview of the ROBINS-I tool

The ROBINS-I tool consists of seven domains that address various sources of bias that may affect the outcomes of non-randomized studies. Each domain is assessed based on specific criteria, leading to an overall risk of bias rating for the study. The ratings for each domain can be classified as low, moderate, serious, or critical risk of bias, reflecting the degree of concern regarding potential biases.

Domains and questions of the ROBINS-I tool

1. **Bias due to confounding**: Is there a potential for confounding factors?
   o **Rating options**: Low risk of bias, moderate risk of bias, serious risk of bias, critical risk of bias, no information.
   o **Assessment**: Evaluate the study design and methods used to control for confounding. A low risk indicates adequate adjustments, while higher risks reflect inadequacies in addressing confounding factors.
2. **Bias in the selection of participants**: Is there a risk of bias in the selection of participants?
   o **Rating options**: Low risk of bias, moderate risk of bias, serious risk of bias, critical risk of bias, no information.

o **Assessment**: Consider the eligibility criteria and enrollment process. A low risk suggests a well-defined selection process, while higher risks indicate potential biases in participant selection.

3. **Bias in the classification of interventions**: Is there a risk of bias in the classification of interventions?
   o **Rating options**: Low risk of bias, moderate risk of bias, serious risk of bias, critical risk of bias, no information.
   o **Assessment**: Assess how interventions were defined and measured. A low risk indicates accurate classification, while higher risks suggest inconsistencies.

4. **Bias due to deviations from intended interventions**: Is there a risk of bias due to deviations from intended interventions?
   o **Rating options**: Low risk of bias, moderate risk of bias, serious risk of bias, critical risk of bias, no information.
   o **Assessment**: Evaluate adherence to the intended interventions. A low risk indicates minimal deviations, while higher risks reflect significant deviations that could affect outcomes.

5. **Bias due to missing data**: Is there a risk of bias due to missing data?
   o **Rating options**: Low risk of bias, moderate risk of bias, serious risk of bias, critical risk of bias, no information.
   o **Assessment**: Consider the extent and handling of missing data. A low risk indicates appropriate handling, while higher risks suggest significant issues with missing data.

6. **Bias in measurement of outcomes**: Is there a risk of bias in the measurement of outcomes?
   o **Rating options**: Low risk of bias, moderate risk of bias, serious risk of bias, critical risk of bias, no information.
   o **Assessment**: Evaluate the methods used to assess outcomes. A low risk indicates reliable measurements, while higher risks suggest potential measurement errors.

7. **Bias in the selection of the reported result**: Is there a risk of bias in the selection of the reported result?
   o **Rating options**: Low risk of bias, moderate risk of bias, serious risk of bias, critical risk of bias, no information.
   o **Assessment**: Assess whether the reported results are selective or incomplete. A low risk indicates comprehensive reporting, while higher risks suggest selective reporting that could distort conclusions.

Overall risk of bias rating

After evaluating each domain, an overall risk of bias rating is assigned to the study. The possible outcomes are:

- **Low risk of bias**: Indicates minimal concerns across all domains.

- **Moderate risk of bias**: Suggests some concerns that may influence findings but not significantly detract from overall conclusions.
- **Serious risk of bias**: Reflects substantial concerns that could seriously affect the validity of the results.
- **Critical risk of bias**: Signifies that the risk of bias severely limits the reliability of the results, leading to questionable conclusions.

Conclusion

The ROBINS-I tool provides a structured and comprehensive framework for assessing the risk of bias in non-randomized studies included in systematic reviews. By systematically evaluating each domain and assigning appropriate ratings, researchers can gain valuable insights into the quality of evidence and the reliability of their conclusions. This rigorous assessment enhances the transparency of systematic reviews and contributes to informed decision-making in clinical and policy contexts. Ultimately, the ROBINS-I tool plays a vital role in ensuring that systematic reviews maintain a high standard of evidence, benefiting the scientific community and stakeholders relying on such evidence for practice and policy.

QUADAS-2

The QUADAS-2 (Quality Assessment of Diagnostic Accuracy Studies) tool is a tool for quality assessment of diagnostic tests accuracy studies. It consists of four domains related to patient selection, index test, reference standard, and flow and timing. Each domain is scored as low, high, or unclear risk of bias, based on the information provided in the study. In addition, a separate domain is used to assess the applicability of the study to the review question.

The QUADAS-2 tool is widely used in systematic reviews and has good inter-rater reliability. However, applying it may be time-consuming and require a detailed understanding of the diagnostic test and the disease being evaluated.

1. Patient selection:
   Answer: Low risk of bias/high risk of bias/unclear risk of bias.
   Evaluate whether the patient selection process is appropriate and unbiased. Consider the eligibility criteria, sampling methods, and potential for bias in patient selection. A low risk of bias indicates that patient selection is adequately addressed. A high risk of bias suggests potential issues in patient selection. An unclear risk of bias indicates insufficient information to assess this domain.
2. Index test:
   Answer: Low risk of bias/high risk of bias/unclear risk of bias.
   Assess the risk of bias in the index test used to assess the target condition. Consider the test methodology, execution, and interpretation. A low risk of bias

indicates a well-performed and validated index test. A high risk of bias suggests potential issues in the index test. An unclear risk of bias indicates insufficient information to assess this domain.

3. Reference standard:

Answer: Low risk of bias/high risk of bias/unclear risk of bias.

Evaluate the risk of bias in the reference standard used to determine the true condition. Consider the standard's validity, execution, and interpretation. A low risk of bias indicates a well-performed and validated reference standard. A high risk of bias suggests potential issues in the reference standard. An unclear risk of bias indicates insufficient information to assess this domain.

4. Flow and timing:

Answer: Low concern/high concern/unclear concern.

Assess the flow and timing of patients throughout the study. Consider whether all patients received the index test and reference standard and if the timing between the tests is appropriate. Low concern indicates that the flow and timing are appropriate and minimize bias. High concern suggests potential issues in patient flow or timing. Unclear concern indicates insufficient information to assess this domain.

Remember to assign a rating for each domain based on the levels of bias or concern indicated. Additionally, evaluate the applicability concerns in each domain, considering whether the study population, index test, reference standard, and patient flow are representative of the intended use of the diagnostic test in practice.

Briefly, The QUADAS-2 tool provides a structured approach to assess the quality and risk of bias in diagnostic accuracy studies. It is important to consider the specific context and limitations of the study when interpreting the findings.

Joanna Briggs Institute

The Joanna Briggs Institute (JBI) has developed various tools for the quality assessment of different studies, including RCTs, qualitative studies, and systematic reviews. These tools are designed to be used as part of the systematic review process, and assess the risk of bias or the strength of evidence for each study included in the review.

The JBI tools are widely used in systematic reviews and have good interrater reliability. They are comprehensive and consider a wide range of potential sources of bias or strength of evidence. However, some of the tools may be time-consuming to apply and may require a detailed understanding of the study design.

JBI critical appraisal checklist for analytical cross-sectional studies

1. Were the criteria for inclusion in the sample clearly defined?
   This question evaluates whether the authors provide clear and specific criteria for selecting study participants, including inclusion and exclusion criteria.
2. Were the study subjects and the setting described in detail?
   This question assesses whether the authors provided sufficient information about the study subjects (e.g., demographics, characteristics) and the study's setting. Detailed descriptions allow for better understanding and comparability of the study population.
3. Was the exposure measured validly and reliably?
   This question examines the method used to measure the exposure variable. Validity refers to whether the measurement accurately captures the intended construct, while reliability assesses the consistency of the measurement. The authors should provide evidence of the validity and reliability of the exposure measurement method.
4. Were objective, standard criteria used for the measurement of the condition?
   This question focuses on whether the authors used objective and standard criteria to measure the condition or outcome of interest. Objective criteria are defined, measurable indicators, while standard criteria are widely accepted and used in the field. Using these criteria helps ensure consistency and comparability of the results.
5. Were confounding factors identified?
   This question examines whether the authors identified potential confounding factors, which are variables that could influence the relationship between the exposure and outcome. Identifying confounding factors is important for accurate interpretation of the study results and adjusting for them in the analysis.
6. Were strategies to deal with confounding factors stated?
   This question assesses whether the authors described strategies to control the confounding factors. Strategies can include matching or stratifying participants based on confounding factors or using statistical methods, such as multivariate regression analysis, to adjust for confounders in the data analysis.
7. Were the outcomes measured in a valid and reliable way?
   This question focuses on the measurement of the outcomes of interest. Validity and reliability of outcome measurements are crucial to ensure accurate assessment. The authors should provide evidence of the validity and reliability of the measurement instruments or methods used.
8. Was appropriate statistical analysis used?
   This question evaluates whether the authors employed appropriate statistical analysis methods to analyze the data. The methods section should provide sufficient detail on the analytical techniques, including regression or stratification methods, and how confounding factors were measured and accounted for.

JBI critical appraisal checklist for case-control studies

JBI instrument could be used to evaluate the quality of case-control studies, including the following items

1. Were the groups comparable other than the presence of disease in cases or the absence of disease in controls?
   Answers: Yes, No, Unclear, or Not/Applicable.
   The control group should represent the source population that produced the cases. Ensure that the study provides clear definitions of the source population and demonstrates comparability between cases and controls in terms of relevant characteristics other than the disease or exposure of interest. Look for information on individual matching, frequency or group matching, or other methods used to establish comparability.

2. Were cases and controls matched appropriately?
   Answers: Yes, No, Unclear, or Not/Applicable.
   Examine how cases and controls were recruited. Determine if the study clearly defines the source population and if participants were selected from the target population, the source population, or a pool of eligible participants. Assess if appropriate matching methods were employed to ensure comparability between cases and controls.

3. Were the same criteria used for the identification of cases and controls?
   Answers: Yes, No, Unclear, or Not/Applicable.
   Determine if the study used clear and specified diagnostic methods or definitions to include cases and controls. Ensure that controls fulfill all the eligibility criteria defined for cases except for the disease diagnosis. Look for evidence of matching by key characteristics if diagnostic methods or definitions were not used.

4. Was exposure measured in a standard, valid, and reliable way?
   Answers: Yes, No, Unclear, or Not/Applicable.
   Examine the study's description of the exposure measurement method. Assess if a validated measurement tool or a gold standard comparison is used to ensure the validity of the exposure measurement. Consider the reliability of the measurement by evaluating processes such as intraobserver and interobserver reliability.

5. Was exposure measured in the same way for cases and controls?
   Answers: Yes, No, Unclear, or Not/Applicable.
   Determine if the study provides a clear description of the exposure measurement method. Ensure that the measurement procedures or protocols are consistent for both cases and controls. Assess if the exposure measures were clearly defined and described in detail.

6. Were confounding factors identified?
   Answers: Yes, No, Unclear, or Not/Applicable.

Confounding factors are differences between comparison groups that can influence the study results. Look for evidence that the study identified potential confounders, such as baseline characteristics, prognostic factors, or concomitant exposures. Assess if the study measured these confounders, where possible, to account for their influence on the study results.

7. Were strategies to deal with confounding factors stated?
   Answer: Yes.
   Evaluate if the study employed strategies to address the effects of confounding factors either in the study design or in data analysis. Look for evidence of matching, stratifying, or adjusting for confounding factors. Review the statistical methods used, such as multivariate regression analysis, to account for the measured confounders.

8. Were outcomes assessed in a standard, valid, and reliable way for cases and controls?
   Answer: Yes.
   Examine the paper's methods section to determine if the outcomes were assessed based on existing definitions or diagnostic criteria. Assess if the measurement tools were validated instruments to ensure validity of outcome assessment. Consider if those involved in data collection were trained or educated in the use of the instruments.

9. Was the exposure period of interest long enough to be meaningful? Answer: Yes.
   Assess if the exposure period specified in the study is appropriate and sufficient to demonstrate an association between the exposure and the outcome. Consider if the exposure period was neither too short nor too long to influence the outcome.

10. Was appropriate statistical analysis used?
    Answer: Yes.
    Evaluate whether the study employed appropriate statistical techniques for data analysis, such as regression or stratification. Assess if the study identified the variables and how they related to the outcome. Consider if the analytical strategy aligns with the assumptions associated with the approach and if it suits the study data.

JBI critical appraisal checklist for case reports

1. Were the patient's demographic characteristics clearly described?
   Answer: Yes/No/Unclear/Not Applicable.
   Evaluate if the case report clearly describes the patient's age, sex, race, medical history, diagnosis, prognosis, previous treatments, past and current diagnostic test results, and medications. Also, assess if the setting and context of the case are adequately described.

2. Was the patient's history clearly described and presented as a timeline?
Answer: Yes/No/Unclear/Not Applicable.
Determine if the case report provides a clear and detailed description of the patient's medical, family, and psychosocial history, including relevant genetic information. Assess if past interventions and their outcomes are clearly presented.

3. Was the current clinical condition of the patient on presentation clearly described?
Answer: Yes/No/Unclear/Not Applicable.
Evaluate if the case report provides a detailed description of the patient's current clinical condition, including the uniqueness of the condition/disease, symptoms, frequency, and severity. Assess if the report indicates whether differential diagnoses were considered.

4. Were diagnostic tests or methods and the results clearly described?
Answer: Yes/No/Unclear/Not Applicable.
Determine if the case report provides sufficient information to understand how the patient was diagnosed. Assess if there is a clear description of the diagnostic tests, including both the gold standard and alternative methods. Look for the inclusion of relevant photographs, illustrations, radiographs, or treatment procedure descriptions when appropriate.

5. Was the intervention(s) or treatment procedure(s) clearly described?
Answer: Yes/No/Unclear/Not Applicable.
Evaluate if the case report clearly describes the intervention or treatment procedures used. Assess if the report provides a detailed description of the treatment/intervention protocol, including the type of treatment, route of administration, dosage, frequency, and potential side effects.

6. Was the postintervention clinical condition clearly described?
Answer: Yes/No/Unclear/Not Applicable.
Determine if the case report clearly describes the patient's clinical condition after the intervention or treatment. Assess if there is a clear indication of the presence or absence of symptoms and if outcomes are presented using images or figures, when appropriate.

7. Were adverse events (harms) or unanticipated events identified and described?
Answer: Yes/No/Unclear/Not Applicable.
Evaluate if the case report identifies and clearly describes any adverse events or harms associated with the treatment or intervention. Assess if the report highlights any unanticipated events that may yield new or useful information.

8. Does the case report provide takeaway lessons?
Answer: Yes/No/Unclear/Not Applicable.
Assess if the case report summarizes key lessons learned, including background information on the condition/disease and clinical practice guidance for clinicians facing similar cases. Look for clear and concise takeaways that provide value and insights to the readers.

JBI critical appraisal checklist for case series

1. Were there clear criteria for inclusion in the case series?
   Answer: Yes/No/Unclear/Not Applicable.
   Evaluate if the case series clearly states the inclusion criteria for study participants. Assess if the criteria are well-defined and detailed and provide all necessary information critical to the study. Consider if exclusion criteria are also specified when appropriate.

2. Was the condition measured in a standard, reliable way for all participants in the case series?
   Answer: Yes/No/Unclear/Not Applicable.
   Determine if the case series clearly describes the measurement method for the condition being studied. Assess if the measurement method is standardized and consistent across all participants, ensuring reliable and repeatable results.

3. Were valid methods used to identify the condition for all participants included in the case series?
   Answer: Yes/No/Unclear/Not Applicable.
   Evaluate if the case series used valid methods for identifying the condition in all participants. Consider if existing definitions or diagnostic criteria were utilized for outcome assessment. Assess if the measurement tools used were validated instruments, as this significantly impacts the validity of outcome assessment.

4. Did the case series have consecutive inclusion of participants?
   Answer: Yes/No/Unclear/Not Applicable.
   Determine if the case series states consecutive inclusion of participants. Assess if the study included all eligible participants in a consecutive manner over a specified period. Look for indications of consecutive inclusion, such as specific time frames or explicit statements.

5. Did the case series have complete inclusion of participants?
   Answer: Yes/No/Unclear/Not Applicable.
   Assess if the case series indicates the complete inclusion of participants. Determine if the study included all eligible participants without any exclusions, ensuring the entire population of interest is represented. Look for explicit statements or descriptions indicating complete inclusion.

6. Was there clear reporting of the demographics of the participants in the study?
   Answer: Yes/No/Unclear/Not Applicable.
   Evaluate if the case series clearly reports relevant participants' demographics, such as age, sex, education, geographic region, ethnicity, and time period. Assess if the demographic information is described in a comprehensive and detailed manner.

7. Was there clear reporting of clinical information of the participants?
   Answer: Yes/No/Unclear/Not Applicable.
   Determine if the case series provides clear reporting of clinical information for participants, including disease status, comorbidities, stage of disease, previous

interventions/treatment, and results of diagnostic tests. Assess if the clinical information is presented in a thorough and detailed manner.

8. Were the outcomes or follow-up results of cases clearly reported?
Answer: Yes/No/Unclear/Not Applicable.
Assess if the case series clearly reports the outcomes or follow-up results of cases. Evaluate if the results of any interventions or treatments are clearly described, including the presence or absence of symptoms. Look for the use of images or figures to convey information effectively. Determine if adverse events, unanticipated events, or new information related to outcomes are identified and described.

9. Was there clear reporting of the presenting site(s)/clinic(s) demographic information?
Answer: Yes/No/Unclear/Not Applicable.
Evaluate if the case series provides clear reporting of demographic information related to the presenting site(s) or clinic(s) where the study was conducted. Determine if relevant details about geographic regions, prevalence, or socio-demographic variables are described sufficiently to allow comparison with other populations of interest.

10. Was statistical analysis appropriate?
Answer: Yes/No/Unclear/Not Applicable.
Consider if the statistical analysis used in the case series was appropriate. Assess if the methods section provides enough detail to identify the specific analytical techniques employed and if they suit the study. Additionally, consider if more appropriate alternate statistical methods could have been used.

JBI Critical Appraisal Checklist for Cohort Studies

1. Were the two groups similar and recruited from the same population?
Answer: Yes/No/Unclear/Not Applicable.
Check if the paper describes participants in both exposed and unexposed groups and determine if they have similar characteristics in relation to the exposure being investigated. Assess if clear inclusion and exclusion criteria were developed before participant recruitment to ensure group similarity.

2. Were the exposures measured similarly to assign people to both exposed and unexposed groups?
Answer: Yes/No/Unclear/Not Applicable.
Evaluate if the study mentions or describes how the exposures were measured. Assess if the exposure measures are clearly defined and described in detail, enabling reviewers to determine if participants received the exposure of interest.

3. Was the exposure measured in a valid and reliable way?
Answer: Yes/No/Unclear/Not Applicable.

Determine if the study clearly describes the method of measuring exposure. Assess if the validity of exposure measurement is addressed, including the availability of a "gold standard" for comparison. Consider if the reliability of exposure measurements, such as intraobserver and interobserver reliability, is discussed.

4. Were confounding factors identified?
Answer: Yes/No/Unclear/Not Applicable.
Assess if the study identifies potential confounding factors, which are differences between the comparison groups that could bias the estimated effect of the exposure investigated. Look for baseline characteristics, prognostic factors, or concomitant exposures that may act as confounders. Evaluate if these factors were measured, where possible.

5. Were strategies to deal with confounding factors stated?
Answer: Yes/No/Unclear/Not Applicable.
Determine if the study describes strategies to address the effects of confounding factors. Assess if matching, stratification, or statistical methods (e.g., multivariate regression analysis) were employed to adjust for confounding factors. Look for a clear description of the statistical methods used to handle confounders.

6. Were the groups/participants free of the outcome at the start of the study (or at the moment of exposure)?
Answer: Yes/No/Unclear/Not Applicable.
Refer to the paper's methods section and assess if the participants were free of the outcomes of interest at the beginning of the study or at the moment of exposure. Look for participant/sample recruitment descriptions, variable definitions, and inclusion/exclusion criteria.

7. Were the outcomes measured in a valid and reliable way?
Answer: Yes/No/Unclear/Not Applicable.
Evaluate if the study describes how the outcomes were measured. Assess if the outcomes are based on existing definitions or diagnostic criteria, indicating validity. Consider if observer-reported or self-reported scales were used, as these may increase the risk of over- or underreporting. Look for the use of validated measurement instruments.

8. Was the follow-up time reported and sufficient to be long enough for outcomes to occur?
Answer: Yes/No/Unclear/Not Applicable.
Assess if the study reports the follow-up time and if it is sufficient for the outcomes to occur. Consider the nature of the population, intervention, disease, or exposure being studied to estimate an appropriate duration of follow-up. Look for multiple papers and expert opinions to determine a suitable follow-up duration.

9. Was follow-up complete, and if not, were the reasons for loss to follow-up described and explored?
Answer: Yes/No/Unclear/Not Applicable.

Evaluate if the study reports a high percentage of follow-up, with at least 80% of participants being followed. Assess if reasons for loss to follow-up are described and explored. Look for clear and justifiable explanations for exclusions, dropouts, or losses to determine if they were comparable in the exposed and unexposed groups.

10. Were strategies to address incomplete follow-up utilized.
Answer: Yes/No/Unclear/Not Applicable.
Consider if the study addresses incomplete follow-up by accounting for participants with unequal follow-up periods in the analysis. Look for adjustment methods that consider differences in the length of follow-up periods, such as using person-years at risk to calculate rates.

11. Was appropriate statistical analysis used?
Answer: Yes/No/Unclear/Not Applicable.
Assess if the study employed appropriate statistical analysis methods. Look for detailed descriptions of the analytical techniques used, particularly regression or stratification methods. Evaluate if the variables included in the analysis and their relationship to the outcome are specified. Consider if the chosen statistical approach aligns with the assumptions associated with the data and research question.

When using this checklist, carefully consider each question and assess the study based on the information provided in the research article. The checklist helps evaluate analytical cross-sectional studies' quality and methodological rigor, facilitating a systematic and evidence-based appraisal process.

Newcastle—Ottawa Scale (NOS)

The Newcastle—Ottawa Scale (NOS) is a tool for quality assessment of nonrandomized studies, such as case-control and cohort studies. It consists of three domains: selection, comparability, and outcome assessment. Each domain is scored as low, moderate, or high risk of bias, based on the information provided in the study. The overall risk of bias is then assessed as low, moderate, or high.

It is easy to use and has good interrater reliability. However, it may not be suitable for all types of observational studies and may not capture all potential sources of bias.

NOS critical appraisal for cross-sectional studies

The NOS checklist is a tool used to assess the quality of nonrandomized studies, such as cross-sectional studies. It consists of three broad categories: selection, comparability, and outcome/exposure. Each category has several items.

1. Selection: (Maximum five stars)
   1.1. Representativeness of the sample:
      (a) Truly representative of the average in the target population. * (all subjects or random sampling)
      (b) Somewhat representative of the average in the target population. * (nonrandom sampling)
      (c) Selected group of users.
      (d) No description of the sampling strategy.
      This question assesses the representativeness of the sample used in the study. Look for studies that use random sampling methods or include all subjects in the target population. Random sampling ensures that the study sample is representative. Nonrandom sampling may introduce selection bias. Selected groups of users may limit generalizability. The lack of a description of the sampling strategy raises concerns about transparency.
   1.2. Sample size:
      (a) Justified and satisfactory. *
      (b) Not justified.
      Consider whether the sample size is appropriate for the research question and objectives. A justified and satisfactory sample size is important for achieving sufficient statistical power. Inadequate sample size may lead to imprecise estimates and limited generalizability. Ensure that the study provides a rationale for the chosen sample size.
   1.3. Nonrespondents:
      (a) Comparability between respondent's and nonrespondents characteristics is established, and the response rate is satisfactory. *
      (b) The response rate is unsatisfactory, or the comparability between respondents and nonrespondents is unsatisfactory.
      (c) No description of the response rate or the characteristics of the responders and the nonresponders.
      Assess the response rate and comparability between respondents and nonrespondents. A satisfactory response rate helps minimize nonresponse bias. The characteristics of respondents and nonrespondents should be comparable to avoid introducing selection bias. Nonresponse bias occurs when nonrespondents differ from respondents in important ways.
   1.4. Ascertainment of the exposure (risk factor):
      (a) Validated measurement tool. **
      (b) Nonvalidated measurement tool, but the tool is available or described. *
      (c) No description of the measurement tool.
      Evaluate the ascertainment of the exposure or risk factor of interest. A validated measurement tool is preferable as it indicates that it has been shown to accurately measure the exposure. Nonvalidated tools may introduce measurement bias. Transparency in describing the measurement tool used is important for assessing the reliability of the exposure assessment.

2. Comparability: (maximum two stars)
The subjects in different outcome groups are comparable, based on the study design or analysis.

    2.1. Confounding factors are controlled.

        (a) The study controls for the most important factor (select one). *

        (b) The study controls for any additional factor. *

        Consider whether the study design or analysis accounts for potential confounding factors. Controlling for the most important factor helps minimize confounding bias. Additional control of other factors increases confidence in the study's findings. Confounding factors are variables that are associated with both the exposure and outcome and may influence the relationship between them.

Data synthesis

Mahsa Ghajarzadeh

Department of Neurology, Johns Hopkins University School of Medicine, Baltimore, MD, United States

What is data synthesis

Data synthesis is defined as combination of a specific set of data that are extracted from individual studies after literature review. The aim of data synthesis is to reach an overall understanding of a problem by collecting, combining, and summarizing the findings of individual studies [1]. As we mentioned previously, all systematic reviews do not include meta-analysis since the synthesis is not possible for all gathered data (when there are no enough data, the results of included studies are very heterogenous, or combination does not make sense).

On the other hand, combination of data of poor-quality studies could be misleading and confusing. If data synthesis is possible, meta-analysis provide explicit, and powerful tool for combing the results of separate studies.

Whether you have meta-analysis in your review, or not, you should have a descriptive table of included studies in your result section of the manuscript including name of the first author of the manuscript, publication year, number of participants, summary of basic characteristics of the participants (age, sex ratio, duration of disease, …), outcomes, and outcome measure. You can also report quality assessment (risk of bias) score of each study in this table (if you do not want to describe in a separate table).

Before conducting data analysis, you should define:

A. Comparisons: determine what changes you desire (changing the score from baseline, changing from the first visit, …), comparing control, and intervention group,..
B. Type of data you desire to include for meta-analysis (categorical or numerical),
C. Summary measures that you are willing to report (pooled mean, pooled standardized mean difference (SMD), odds ratio (OR), risk ratio (RR), ..).

What is meta-analysis and why it is useful?

Meta-analysis is the statistical combination of weighted effect sizes of individual studies [2].

Systematic Review and Meta-Analysis. https://doi.org/10.1016/B978-0-443-13428-9.00009-4

Effect measures or measures of association are the method of describing the outcome of individuals who participated in the study (for instance mean change in weight after a diet, odds of developing cancer following a certain intervention, ..).

Decisions about the outcomes of interest for analysis, comparisons, and summary effects should be addressed in the protocol, but it is possible to be changed after data extraction.

How meta-analysis may help us?

Combining the results of separate studies using meta-analysis improves precision, increases the number of included participants, and reduces random error. It also provides a better chance to detect a real effect by improving statistical power.

It also helps:

A. Assessing the heterogeneity between the results of included studies,
B. Exploration of the pattern of the findings across included studies,
C. Narrowing confidence interval,
D. Showing gap of knowledge (for example no results from a specific outcome from studies,..) [3].

The results of your meta-analysis could be misleading if you do not pay attention to:

A. Your review question and its components,
B. Your inclusion, and exclusion criteria,
C. Critical appraisal of included studies,
D. Collecting data in properly and accurately,
E. Heterogeneity between the results of included studies.

The summary estimate reflects the best guess of the effect size, and also shows the best direction of the effect size in the systematic reviews of interventional studies.

For each pooled effect size, the confidence interval is reported to show the uncertainty around the estimate. The narrower the confidence interval, the more precise the estimate.

Types of data

1. Dichotomous/binary outcomes, which have two distinct levels (e.g., sex (male, female), death (yes/no)), and the results usually be summarized as frequency, or proportion.
2. Continuous outcomes, which consists of a measurement on a numerical scale, and can take many decimals (e.g., weight, height, blood pressure), besides the results usually be summarized as mean and standard deviation (SD), or median and interquartile range (IQR).

3. Ordinal outcomes, which have categories that rank their orders (e.g., stage of the disease (I, II, III, IV). Their results can be presented as frequency, or proportion.

Based on the outcome of the interest, we use different summary or pooled effect measures to report the results.

For binary outcomes such as developing MS or not, you could report pooled odds ratio (odds), risk ratio (RR) or risk difference (RD), or we could report pooled frequency (prevalence/incidence).

For continuous variables such as weight we can apply pooled mean or if we want to compare weight before and after a certain treatment, we can apply mean change (MC), and standardized mean difference (SMD), or mean difference (MD) (They will be discussed in details later in this chapter).

For categorical data, the best way for analysis is to dichotomize them, and then apply methods for pooling the dichotomous variables.

To get an overall summary estimate, weighted averages of individual estimates are combined. The greater the weight of a study, the more influence of that study on overall study.

For all effect sizes, the following formula work:

$$\text{Weighted average} = \text{sum of (estimate} \times \text{weight) /sum of weights} = \Sigma\, Y_i\, W_i\, /\, \Sigma\, W_i$$

$$\text{Inverse of Variance weight} = 1\, /\, \text{sum of weights} = 1/\, \Sigma W i$$

Y_i = Effect size estimate in the ith study.
W_i = Weight, which is given to the ith study.

Heterogeneity
Heterogeneity will be discussed in details in Chapter 13

Variation between the results of included studies is inevitable, some arise only from random error (which could be removed by increasing the sample size of studies) and some arise from statistical heterogeneity between the results of included studies, which indicates methodological or clinical differences between included studies [3].

The poor overlap between confidence intervals of individual effect sizes in the forest plot, may reflect heterogeneity between results of the studies.

The most common statistic that is used to quantify the heterogeneity is I^2, which ranges from 0% to 100% [4]. I^2 values less than 50% show low levels of heterogeneity, while higher values indicate higher levels of heterogeneity [4].

When the statistical heterogeneity is high among the studies, one approach is to select random effects model for meta-analysis (instead of fixed effects model). So, we are going to discuss fixed versus random effects model here. In Fig. 9.1, the I^2 is zero which shows no statistical heterogeneity in the meta-analysis (CI of included studies has good overlap) (Fig. 9.1).

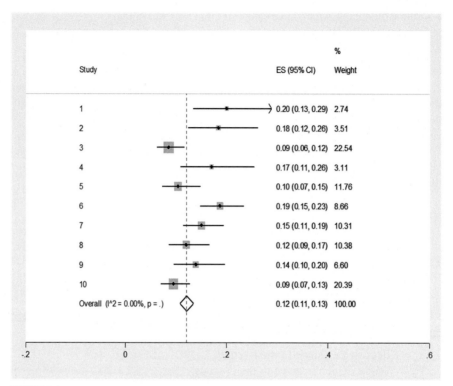

FIGURE 9.1

The pooled prevalence obtained by fixed effects model.

Two statistical models are commonly used for meta-analysis

A. Fixed-effects model: It assumes that there is one true effect size which could be observed across all studies, and variability between the included studies is due to chance. So, under this model, there is only one source of variance, which is random error inherited in each study, and the assumption is that there is no between study variability. This model considers only within studies variability as the source of total variability, and weights the contribution of each study to the amount of information provided by the study. So, larger studies will have greater weights [5].

$$\text{Weight of each study} = 1/v_i,$$

$$\text{Summary effect} = \Sigma\, Y_i\, W_i\, /\, \Sigma\, W_i$$

B. Random-effects: This model allows variability between the results of studies, and also a distribution for the true effect size. By this model, the variability that is seen is due to chance (within studies), and also between study variability. This model weights each study using a combination of variance of between and withing studies. Applying this model, larger studies will not have higher weights [5].

The reason why under the random-effects model weights of larger studies are smaller than the weights under the fixed-effects model is the way we weight each study.

In the fixed effects model the weight of each study is $1/v_i$ while under the random effects model the weight of each study is $1/v_i + T^2$ (T^2 is between study variance) (Fig. 9.2).

Comparing Fig. 9.1 and 9.2 you can see that, the weight of study numbe r3 is higher in Fig. 9.1 than Fig. 9.2 (larger study got higher weight in fixed effect model than random effect model) and the confidence interval for the summary effect obtained by random-effects model is wider than the fixed-effects model (95% CI:11-16 vs 11-13).

Also, the study weights are more similar under random-effects model.

Under the fixed-effects model, each study has its unique variance (v_i), but under the random effects model the variance of each study is ($v_i + T^2$) (V_i is each study unique variance, and T^2 is between-study variance, which is common to all studies)

If T^2 is estimated to be zero, then fixed-effects model should be considered.

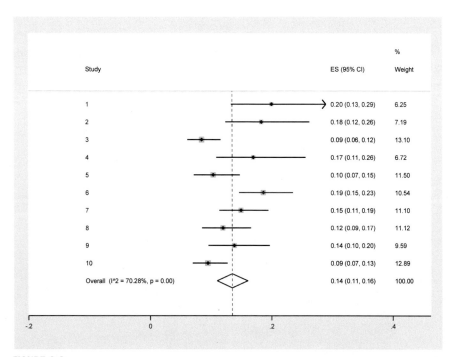

FIGURE 9.2

The pooled prevalence obtained by random effects model.

OSummary estimates

Odds ratio (OR)

OR is commonly used to express dichotomous outcomes.

An odds ratio is a measure of association between a potential risk factor and the outcome [6]. It reflects the odds of the event in one group (e.g., exposed) versus the odds of the event in the other group (nonexposed). It can take any value between zero and infinity.

Imagine that you have two groups: one group is living in an area with air pollution, and the other group is living in a place with fresh air. If you want to report the odds of developing lung cancer in these groups, you can divide the odds of the first group by the second group.

OR = odds in the exposed group/odds in the nonexposed group.
OR = 1 Exposure does not affect the odds of outcome
OR>1 Exposure associated with higher odds of outcome
OR<1 Exposure associated with lower odds of outcome

We show an example of calculating OR in two groups: exposed: air pollution, event: lung cancer (Table 9.1).

$$OR = \frac{40/60}{20/80} = 2.66$$

OR is higher than 1, indicating that odds of developing lung cancer is 2.66-fold higher in people who are living in places with air pollution than people who are living in places with fresh air.

Odds ratios could be combined using inverse variance method.

For pooling ORs, we need log(OR), and also SE of log(OR).

$$\ln(OR) = \ln(ad \, / \, bc)$$

$$SE\{\ln(OR)\} = \sqrt{\frac{1}{a} + \frac{1}{b} + \frac{1}{c} + \frac{1}{d}}$$

For the above example:

$$\ln(2.66) = 0.97$$

$$SE(\ln(OR)) = \sqrt{0.1035} = 0.3217$$

Table 9.1 Data regarding exposure and outcome (air pollution as an exposure and lung cancer as an outcome).

	Event	No-event
Exposed	40	60
Unexposed	20	80

Different methods such as inverse variance, Peto, Mante-Haenszel under the fixed effects model, and DerSimonian Laird under the random effects model could be used for combining ORs.

Risk ratio (RR)

RR is an indicator, which is used for binary outcomes.

The risk ratio (RR) is the probability of an event in one group divided by the probability of an event in another group. (Probability is total number of events divided by total number of participants).

RR=Risk in one group/Risk in another group.

For above example if we want to calculate RR:

$$RR = \frac{40/100}{20/100} = 2.$$

RR $= 1$, Exposure does not affect the outcome,

RR > 1, The risk of the outcome is increased by the exposure

RR < 1, The risk of the outcome is decreased by the exposure

When the event is rare, OR and RR are approximately equal.

OR is always more extreme than RR (more away from the null value, 1), and is assumed that OR overestimates (OR>1) the relationship or underestimates (OR<1).

Like ORs, RRs could be combined using inverse variance method, by applying its ln, and SE.

$$Ln\ (RR) = \ln(a\ /\ (a+b)\ /\ c\ /\ (c+d))$$

$$SE\{\ln(RR)\} = \sqrt{\frac{1}{a} + \frac{1}{c} - \frac{1}{a+b} - \frac{1}{c+d}}$$

For this example:

$$\ln(RR) = \ln(2) = 0.69$$

$$SE_{\ln}(1\ /\ 40 + 1\ /\ 20 - 1\ /\ 100 - 1\ /\ 100) = 0.055$$

Different methods such as inverse variance, and Mante-Haenszel under the fixed effects model, and DerSimonian Laird under the random effects model could be used for combining RRs.

Risk difference (RD)

The risk difference (RD) is the risk in one group minus the risk in the other group.

If RD $= 0$, the two groups are equal regarding the risk of interest.

It should be considered that if 95% CI of RD includes 0, then the risk difference is not statistically significant.

$$RD = \frac{a}{a+b} - \frac{c}{c+d}$$

$$SE\{RD\} = \sqrt{\frac{a \times b}{(a+b)^3} + \frac{c \times d}{(c+d)^3}}$$

For the example the RD would be:

$$RD = 40/100 - 20/100 = 0.2$$

$$SE(RD) = 0.63$$

This can show that the risk of the event in exposed group is 20% higher than the nonexposed group.

Continuous data

Continuous variables are outcomes such as weight, height, and blood pressure that take values with decimals (the assumption is that the continuous outcomes have a normal distribution in each arm of the study). Continuous data are usually summarized as mean, and variation around the mean using standard deviation (SD) or standard error (SE).

Imagine we had four studies and participants were followed up for 8 weeks after administrating a certain type of treatment. The mean weight gains, which are reported in studies, are as follow: 4, 6, 2, 5 kg. So, the average of weight gain is 3.75 kg. We can conclude that on average, this treatment results in 3.75 kg weight gain after 8 weeks of administration.

Meta-analysis averages the data correspondingly, except that precise values of the mean (from included studies), are given larger weightage during meta-analysis, and pooling the results [7].

For continuous variables, standard error of mean (SEM) is the determinant of precision (once the standard deviation is small or the sample size is large, SEM is small, indicating greater precision (SEM $= \frac{SD}{\sqrt{n}}$).

Larger SD (wide scatter of individual values) shows a wide margin of error, resulting in larger SEM, indicating that the sample mean is not a true representation of population mean [7]. Larger SEM corresponds to wider CIs around the mean.

To evaluate the effects of an intervention on continuous outcome in various groups, absolute difference between the mean values (mean difference) could be reported. And if the units are not the same in different studies, standardized mean difference (SMD) could be used.

To pool means, we need each mean value, as well as SE for each mean.

Mean difference (MD)

MD is the absolute difference between mean values of two groups or mean change of a group in two time periods. It is the appropriate effect measure for continuous variables especially once the scale is the same in included studies.

If mean value in one group is 10, and in other group is 6.5, then the MD would be 3.5, signifying that the outcome is 3.5 units bigger in the first group.

MD $= 0$, means there is no difference between two groups.
MD > 1, experiment group experienced an increase in the outcome value,
MD < 1, experiment group experienced a decrease in the outcome value.

If the 95% CI of MD includes 0, it shows that the difference between two groups is not significant.

$$MD = Mean_1 - mean_2$$

$$SE_{MD} = \sqrt{\frac{s_1^2}{N_1} + \frac{s_2^2}{N_2}}$$

Standardized mean difference (SMD)

When the outcome of interest in included studies is reported in different units (such as kg, and gr or cm and inches), it is logical to use SMDs to pool mean differences.

For instance, if some studies reported the effect of a specific diet in kilograms and others reported body mass index (BMI) as the outcome of interest we can use SMD, or when different studies used various questionnaires to evaluate quality of life.

When we divide the mean difference by the pooled SD, we get SMD that shows mean difference in the units of SD.

To calculate the pooled SMD, we can use different denominators (pooled SD).
The pooled SD could be calculated in three ways:

A. Cohen's d pooled SD:

$$Pooled\ SD = \sqrt{\frac{(SD_1^2 + SD_2^2)}{2}}$$

B. Hedge's g pooled SD:

$$s_p = \sqrt{\frac{(n_1 - 1)s_1^2 + (n_2 - 1)s_2^2}{2}}$$

C. Glass's Δ pooled SD:

In this case, you use the control's group SD as the pooled SD in the formula. This method is recommended when we have more than one experimental group, and only a control group. Although, it uses only one SD and is easy to apply, it is not very accurate [8].

For interpretation SMD this guidance is used:

1. SMD values between 0.2 and 0.5 are considered small,
2. SMD values between 0.5 and 0.8 are considered medium,
3. SMD values between more than 0.8 are considered large [7].

It is obvious that SMD equal to zero means that there is no difference between mean scores of two groups, and if the 95% confidence interval of SMD includes zero, it shows that the difference is not statistically significant.

Important notes

A. When the sample size is less than 20, Cohen's d overestimates the true effect size, so Hedge's g is recommended for pooling SDs.
B. For all data analysis consider that if some cells are zero in your table, some softwares add 0.5 to 0 cells, but this approach will:
   a. Bias the estimates towards no difference between the study groups,
   b. Overestimates the variance.

If you do not want to add 0.5 to your cells, for calculating pooled OR/RR you can exclude such studies from your meta-analysis.

The below figure is a sample of forest plot that shows SMD of each study and also pooled SMD.

The square, which is located in the center of each line, shows the point estimate of each study and the horizontal line indicates the confidence interval of the that point estimate.

The size of the square reflects the size of the study population (larger studies have larger squares). T should be noted that longer lines of confidence intervals indicate less accurate effect estimate (Fig. 9.3).

This figure shows that the first study has the biggest square, reflecting larger sample size and the highest weight among all other included studies.

The diamond at the bottom of the figure reflects the pooled estimate (the point that the larger diameter crosses the line (0.59)), while the smaller diameter shows the confidence interval of the pooled estimate (0.52—0.66) (Table 9.2).

The variability between the results of included studies is called heterogeneity, which could have four sources:

A. Clinical: Variability between the participants,
B. Logical: Variability between the design of the studies,

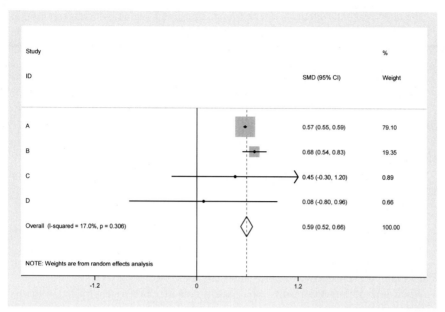

FIGURE 9.3

Forest plot showing SMDs of different studies.

C. Quality: Variability between the quality of studies,
D. Statistical: Variability between results of the included studies, which is more than chance alone [9].

First of all, evaluate the forest plot to see if the confidence intervals of included studies have overlaps or not. Poor overlap between the CIs, indicate high heterogeneity and variability in estimation.

Table 9.2 Different methods of combining.

	Fixed effects model	**Random effects model**
Continuous outcomes Mean difference Standardized mean difference	Inverse variance (IV) Inverse variance (IV)	
Odds ratio	Mantel-Haenszel Peto exact Inverse variance (IV)	DerSimonian-Laird
Risk ratio (RR)	Mantel-Haenszel Inverse variance (IV)	DerSimonian-Laird
Risk difference (RD)	Inverse variance (IV)	DerSimonian-Laird

The degree of heterogeneity can be found regarding I^2 value, which is reported in forest plots. I^2 shows the percentage of total variation between the results of the studies, which is due to heterogeneity not chance and could be ranged between 0% and 100%.

Higher the I^2, greater heterogeneity between the results of the studies.

I2 more than 75% is considered high and arise more precision.

When I2 is more than 50%, you can apply random effects model to combine the results of included studies.

But, it is very important to investigate the source of the heterogeneity and try to solve it.

To identify the source of the heterogeneity, you can do subgroup analysis or meta-regression.

Some important points:

1. If studies report the same outcome but, in different time points, it is not appropriate to combine the results.
2. The best way to present the results is drawing a Forest plot. It includes point estimate of each study as well as summary estimate.
3. When interpreting the results, you should consider heterogeneity index of the summary results (will be discussed later).

References

[1] Gurevitch J, Koricheva J, Nakagawa S, Stewart G. Meta-analysis and the science of research synthesis. Nature 2018;555(7695):175−82.

[2] Crombie IK, Davies HT. What is meta-analysis. What is 2009;1(8).

[3] Reviews Cf, Dissemination. CRD's guidance for undertaking reviews in healthcare. York Publ. Services; 2009.

[4] Borenstein M, Higgins JP, Hedges LV, Rothstein HR. Basics of meta-analysis: I2 is not an absolute measure of heterogeneity. Res Synth Methods 2017;8(1):5−18.

[5] Borenstein M, Hedges LV, Higgins JP, Rothstein HR. A basic introduction to fixed-effect and random-effects models for meta-analysis. Res Synth Methods 2010;1(2):97−111.

[6] Tenny S, Hoffman MR. Odds ratio. 2017.

[7] Andrade C. Mean difference, standardized mean difference (SMD), and their use in meta-analysis: as simple as it gets. J Clin Psychiatr 2020;81(5):11349.

[8] Norman GR, Streiner DL. Biostatistics: the bare essentials: PMPH USA. BC Decker; 2008.

[9] Boland ACM, Dickson R, editors. Doing a systematic review a student's guide. 2nd ed. SAGE Publications Inc.; p. 148.

Performing meta-analysis in different softwares

10

Mahsa Ghajarzadeh

Department of Neurology, Johns Hopkins University School of Medicine, Baltimore, MD, United States

To conduct meta-analysis, we can use different softwares. In this chapter, we will introduce various software for meta-analysis and will discuss different samples.

STATA

One of the most commonly used softwares for-meta-analysis is STATA.

We can pool different effect sizes such as prevalence rates, incidence rates, standardized mean differences (SMDs), odds ratios (ORs), and risk ratios (RRs) in STATA.

In this book we have focused on an example in different chapters (the prevalence of RLS [Restless leg syndrome] in patients with MS). In this chapter we will go through this example to pool the prevalence of RLS in patients with MS as well as other examples to learn how to do meta-analysis using various softwares.

For pooling the prevalence rates of RLS in patients with MS, we have an synthetisized data sheet, which is displayed below. The first column shows the name of the authors, the second column shows the total number of patients with MS, and the third column displays number of patients with RLS (Fig. 10.1).

The general preface of STATA includes Review, Results, Command, and Variables windows (Fig. 10.2).

For incidence and prevalence meta-analysis, you need the command metaprop.

For meta-analysis of other effect sizes (such as standardized mean difference, odds ratio, risk ratio), we need metan command.

Meta-analysis commands are not included in STATA by default, so we have to install the commands [1].

To pool prevalence rates from different studies, in the command section of STATA, you have to type the following command:

```
metaprop RLS TotalMS, random label (namevar=Author).
```

Metaprop is the command which is used to pool prevalence rates or incidence rates. In this example,RLS is the number of patients with MS who had RLS, TotalMS is the total number of patients with MS, random is random effects model

	Author	TotalMS	RLS
1	AA	100	23
2	BB	115	22
3	CC	48	10
4	DD	96	26
5	EE	345	129
6	FF	178	50
7	GG	35	5
8	HH	128	20
9	II	183	45
10	JJ	2200	870

FIGURE 10.1

The spreadsheet of STATA.

FIGURE 10.2

Default interface of STATA.

for pooling data, which is recommended for pooling prevalence and incidence rates (Instead of fixed effects model), and label is the option to show the name of the first authors of each study.

```
. metaprop RLS TotalMS, random label(namevar= Author)

              Study     |    ES    [95% Conf. Interval]     % Weight
--------------------------+----------------------------------------------
AA                        |    0.23      0.16         0.32     9.80
BB                        |    0.19      0.13         0.27    10.15
CC                        |    0.21      0.12         0.34     8.63
DD                        |    0.27      0.19         0.37     9.57
EE                        |    0.37      0.32         0.43    10.75
FF                        |    0.28      0.22         0.35    10.33
GG                        |    0.14      0.06         0.29     8.59
HH                        |    0.16      0.10         0.23    10.42
II                        |    0.25      0.19         0.31    10.44
JJ                        |    0.40      0.38         0.42    11.33
--------------------------+----------------------------------------------
Random pooled  ES         |    0.25      0.19         0.32   100.00
--------------------------+----------------------------------------------

   Heterogeneity chi^2 =      116.08 (d.f. = 9) p =        0.00
   I^2 (variation in ES attributable to heterogeneity) =    92.25%
   Estimate of between-study variance Tau^2 =        0.01

   Test of ES=0 : z=       7.32 p =        0.00
```

FIGURE 10.3

The table of the results of pooling the prevalence of RLS in patients with MS in STATA.

After typing the command, press enter, then you will get the following table in the results section (Fig. 10.3).

As you can see in the obtained results, the estimates (prevalence of RLS in patients with MS) (under the ES column) for each study range between 0.14(14%) and 0.4(40%), and the pooled prevalence is estimated as 25% (95% CI: 19%–32%).

You can also see heterogeneity Chi square as 116.08, and its corresponding P-value as <.001.

I^2 (which shows variation in estimate, which is attributed to heterogeneity between study results not due to chance) is estimated as 92.25% in this meta-analysis.

The between-study variance, which is shown by Tau^2 is estimated as 0.01 (we will discuss about the heterogeneity in Chapter 13).

At the bottom line, you see test of estimate using standard score as $z = 7.32$, and P value less than 0.001 (showing that the pooled prevalence is significantly higher than 0).

The results are also displayed as a Frost plot (Fig. 10.4).

Each square in front of each individual study represents the point estimate of the corresponding study, and the horizontal line corresponds to the confidence interval of the effect size of the study.

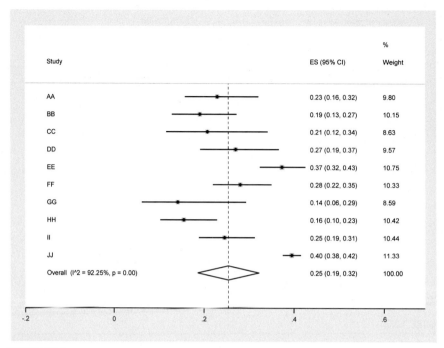

FIGURE 10.4

The forest-plot showing the pooled prevalence of RLS in patients with MS.

The diamond at the bottom of the forest plot shows the pooled effect size, and the width of the diamond represents the 95% confidence interval around the pooled estimate.

We will discuss more about the forest plot in Chapter 11.

For pooling incidences, the STATA command is exactly the same as the command for pooling prevalence rates.

Pooling standardized mean differences (SMDs)

The standardized mean difference (SMD) is the difference between two means in the unit of standard deviation (SD) (not its original unit). For example, when we want to compare weights a spesific regimen in different studies, but the wieghts are reported in kilograms in some studies and in pounds in the other studies. So, we can apply SMDs to compare weights after the intervention in included studies (SMDs of 0.2, 0.5, and 0.8 are conventionally considered to be small, medium, and large, respectively) [2].

Think that you desire to compare the mean difference of vitamin d level in patients with diabetes and healthy controls. The generated data for this example are displayed in the following spreadsheet (Fig. 10.5).

var1	NO1	mean1	sd1	NO2	mean2	sd2
AA	100	30	10	100	42	8.5
BB	130	26.5	9	120	34	6.5
CC	200	32	8.7	200	40.2	11
DD	190	30.7	9.7	180	40.2	10.2
EE	170	16.9	7.7	180	28	10.9
FF	89	35	10	98	40.4	9.8
GG	98	30	8	110	37	7
HH	65	15	4	160	29	10
II	70	18	6	78	17	9
JJ	300	17.7	5.6	300	14.6	5.7

FIGURE 10.5

Spreadsheet for pooling SMDs.

For pooling standardized mean differences (SMDs), you have to have the number of participants in each study group, and also mean and standard deviation of vitamin d level in each group in every single included study (in this example, NO1 (number of patients), mean1, and sd1 correspond to diabetic group, and NO2,mean2, sd2 correspond to the control group).

STATA command for pooling (SMDs) is as follow:

```
metan NO1 mean1 sd1 NO2 mean2 sd2, random label (namevar= var1)
```

The pooled SMD is estimated as -0.76(95% CI: -1.22, -0.3) ($I^2 = 97.2\%$, $P < .001$) (Fig. 10.6A).

The pooled SMD as -0.76 shows that the pooled mean of vitamin d level in diabetic group is 0.76 sd below the mean of the control group.

When you type label, the vertical axis of the graph shows the study IDs.

If you do not type random, the pooled estimate would becalculated under the fixed effects model (Fig. 10.6B).

To pool the SMDs of the included studies differently, you could calculate the pooled SMD by subtracting the SMDs of the control group from those of the case group. The command for this would be:

```
metan NO2 mean2 sd2 NO1 mean1 sd1, random label (namevar= var1)
```

This time the pooled SMD will be 0.76 (95% CI: 0.3−1.22), which shows that the pooled mean in control group is 0.76 SD above the mean of the diabetic group (Fig. 10.7).

Typically, we apply random effects model for pooling data when the percent of heterogeneity is higher than 50%.

After running command metan, six columns will be added to the end of the dataset, which includes the total sample size of the study (NO1+NO2) which is shown as _SS, effect size of each study(_ES), standard error of the effect size(_seES), lower and upper limits of CI for the estmate (LCI,UCI), and the weight of the study in the nalysis (WT) (Fig. 10.8).

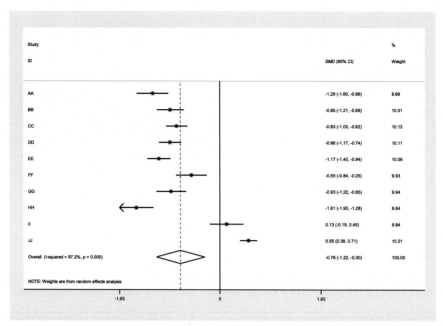

FIGURE 10.6A

Forest plot of the pooled SMD of vitamin d level using random effects model.

```
           Study    |    SMD    [95% Conf. Interval]    % Weight
  ------------------+----------------------------------------------
           AA       | -1.293    -1.598    -0.988          6.29
           BB       | -0.949    -1.211    -0.688          8.54
           CC       | -0.827    -1.031    -0.623         14.03
           DD       | -0.955    -1.170    -0.740         12.63
           EE       | -1.171    -1.398    -0.944         11.36
           FF       | -0.546    -0.838    -0.253          6.85
           GG       | -0.935    -1.222    -0.648          7.11
           HH       | -1.607    -1.932    -1.282          5.55
           II       |  0.129    -0.194     0.452          5.61
           JJ       |  0.549     0.386     0.712         22.02
  ------------------+----------------------------------------------
  I-V pooled SMD    | -0.597    -0.674    -0.521        100.00
  ------------------+----------------------------------------------

     Heterogeneity chi-squared = 318.80 (d.f. = 9) p = 0.000
     I-squared (variation in SMD attributable to heterogeneity) =  97.2%

     Test of SMD=0 : z=  15.30 p = 0.000
```

FIGURE 10.6B

The pooled SMD of vitamin d level using fixed effect model.

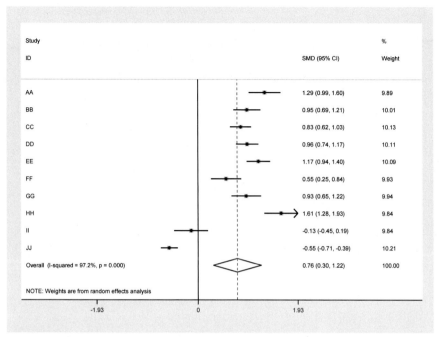

FIGURE 10.7

The pooled SMD (control group − case group) using random effect model.

To obtain funnel plot, type the following command:

```
Metafunnel _ES _seES
```

When you see that the funnel plot is asymmetric, you have to apply tests to evaluate publication bias (egger's or beg tests) (Figs. 10.9−10.11).

To obtain these results, type the following command:

```
metabias _ES _seES, egger
```

To evluate if publication bias exists or not, you can see the corresponding *P*-value of bias is 0.079 which indicates that there is no evidence of publication bias.

To obtain the results of Begg test, you have to type the following command:

```
metabias _ES _seES, begg
```

The corresponding *P* value for the Begg test is 0.421, indicating that there is no evidence for publication bias.

Pooling odds ratios (ORs)

If you want to find the pooled odds of developing MS, which is related to vitamin d deficiency, you have to extract the odds ratios and their corresponding confidence intervals from included studies (lower limit of CI, and upper limit of CI). Below, you can find generated data that for this meta-analysis:

	var1	NO1	mean1	sd1	NO2	mean2	sd2	_SS	_ES	_seES	_LCI	_UCI	_WT
1	AA	100	30	10	100	42	8.5	200	-1.293054	.1556348	-1.598053	-.9880153	9.894328
2	BB	130	26.5	9	120	34	6.5	250	-.9493956	.1335773	-1.211202	-.687589	10.00769
3	CC	200	32	8.7	200	40.2	11	400	-.826871	.1042062	-1.031111	-.6226305	10.13482
4	DD	190	30.7	9.7	180	40.2	10.2	370	-.9551246	.1098098	-1.170348	-.7399012	10.11276
5	EE	170	16.9	7.7	180	28	10.9	350	-1.17066	.1157883	-1.397601	-.9437187	10.08807
6	FF	89	35	10	98	40.4	9.8	187	-.5456951	.1491471	-.838018	-.2533721	9.929191
7	GG	98	30	8	110	37	7	208	-.9348877	.1463434	-1.221715	-.64806	9.943871
8	HH	65	15	4	160	29	10	225	-1.607048	.1656056	-1.931629	-1.282467	9.838371
9	II	70	18	6	78	17	9	148	.1293878	.1648137	-.1936412	.4524167	9.842918
10	JJ	300	17.7	5.6	300	14.6	5.7	600	.5486512	.0831766	.3856279	.7116744	10.20798

FIGURE 10.8

The preface of the dataset in STATA.

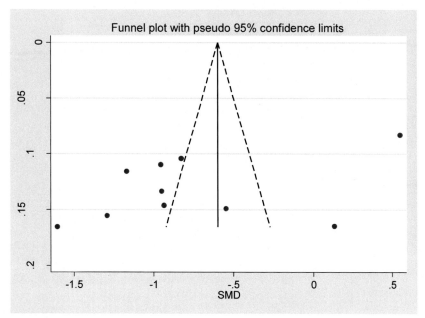

FIGURE 10.9

The funnel plot.

```
Note: data input format theta se_theta assumed.

Egger's test for small-study effects:
Regress standard normal deviate of intervention
effect estimate against its standard error

Number of studies =  10                       Root MSE      =   5.145

    Std_Eff |    Coef.    Std. Err.    t    P>|t|    [95% Conf. Interval]
------------+------------------------------------------------------------
      slope |  1.141093   .8875132   1.29   0.235    -.9055158   3.187702
       bias | -14.45812   7.190532  -2.01   0.079    -31.03952   2.123275


Test of H0: no small-study effects        P = 0.079
```

FIGURE 10.10

The results of Egger's test for SMDs.

Note: data input format theta se_theta assumed.

Begg's test for small-study effects:
Rank correlation between standardized intervention effect and its standard error

adj. Kendall's Score (P-Q) =   -9
       Std. Dev. of Score = 11.18
       Number of Studies =   10
                       z =   -0.80
               Pr > |z| =   0.421
                       z =   0.72 (continuity corrected)
               Pr > |z| =   0.474 (continuity corrected)

FIGURE 10.11

The results of Begg test for pooled ORs.

	Author	OR	LL	UL
1	AA	2.1	1.3	4
2	BB	1.89	.9	6.4
3	CC	2	.9	3.1
4	DD	1.7	1.3	3.2
5	EE	.8	.6	2.5
6	FF	3.7	2	4.3
7	GG	4.2	3.1	6.8
8	HH	1.9	1.1	4
9	II	.7	.6	1.7
10	JJ	2.9	1.8	4

FIGURE 10.12

The STATA spreadsheet of ORs and their corresponding CIs.

The STATA spreadsheet would be as follows (Fig. 10.12):

For pooling ORs and RRs (risk ratios), you have to obtain natural logarithm (ln) values of ORs/RRs, and also ln of lower and upper limits of corresponding CIs.

To obtain ln, you need to type the following command in STATA:

```
gen lnOR=ln(OR)
```

To obtain ln of lower and upper limits of the confidence interval,
You have to type the following commands:

```
gen llor=ln(LL)
gen ulor=ln(UL)
```

	Author	OR	LL	UL	LnOR	llor	ulor
1	AA	2.1	1.3	4	.7419373	.2623642	1.386294
2	BB	1.89	.9	6.4	.6365768	-.1053605	1.856298
3	CC	2	.9	3.1	.6931472	-.1053605	1.131402
4	DD	1.7	1.3	3.2	.5306283	.2623642	1.163151
5	EE	.8	.6	2.5	-.2231435	-.5108256	.9162908
6	FF	3.7	2	4.3	1.308333	.6931472	1.458615
7	GG	4.2	3.1	6.8	1.435084	1.131402	1.916923
8	HH	1.9	1.1	4	.6418539	.0953102	1.386294
9	II	.7	.6	1.7	-.356675	-.5108256	.5306283
10	JJ	2.9	1.8	4	1.064711	.5877866	1.386294

FIGURE 10.13

The spreadsheet of new added variables in STATA.

After typing and entering above commands in STATA, you will have three new variable columns in STATA, which are displayed at the end of the datasheet (LnOR, llor, ulor) (Fig. 10.13).

To pool ORs, you have to write the following command in the command window of STATA:

```
metan LnOR llor ulor, eform
```

As you applied logarithmic values, you have to use eform option to obtain exponentiated results for pooled OR/RR.

The results of the above command are as follows (Fig. 10.14):

The OR of each individual study is presented under ES column, and the corresponding weight is shown under the weight column.

As the results show, the pooled OR is 2.26 with 95% CI as 1.93—2.65.

The forest plot of this meta-analysis would be as follows (Fig. 10.15).

The heterogeneity between results of included study based on I^2 is 80.9%.

For pooling the risk ratios (RRs), you can follow the same method you applied for pooling the ORs (you have to type this command: metan lnrr lnll lnul, eform).

Pooling ORs/RRs using original data

When you want to pool ORs or RRs, sometimes the original studies did not provide crude ORs/RRs and their corresponding CIs. So, you have to extract data from two by two tables. We need number of exposed individuals who developed the disease (a), number of exposed individuals without the disease (b), number of nonexposed individuals with the disease (c), and number of nonexposed individuals without the disease (d) (Fig. 10.16).

```
.
.
.
. metan LnOR llcr ulor, eform label(namevar= Author)

              Study    |     ES    [95% Conf. Interval]     % Weight
    ---------------------+------------------------------------------------
    AA                   |   2.100     1.300      4.000         8.04
    BB                   |   1.890     0.900      6.400         2.64
    CC                   |   2.000     0.900      3.100         6.64
    DD                   |   1.700     1.300      3.200        12.52
    EE                   |   0.800     0.600      2.500         4.99
    FF                   |   3.700     2.000      4.300        17.33
    GG                   |   4.200     3.100      6.800        16.46
    HH                   |   1.900     1.100      4.000         6.09
    II                   |   0.700     0.600      1.700         9.36
    JJ                   |   2.900     1.800      4.000        15.93
    ---------------------+------------------------------------------------
    I-V pooled ES        |   2.262     1.928      2.652       100.00
    ---------------------+------------------------------------------------
    Heterogeneity calculated by formula
      Q = SIGMA_i{ (1/variance_i)*(effect_i - effect_pooled)^2 }
    where variance_i = ((upper limit - lower limit)/(2*z))^2

      Heterogeneity chi-squared =  47.19 (d.f. = 9) p = 0.000
      I-squared (variation in ES attributable to heterogeneity) =  80.9%

      Test of ES=1 : z=  10.04 p = 0.000

.
```

FIGURE 10.14

Results of pooling ORs in STATA.

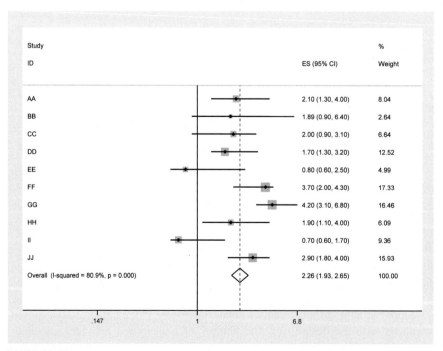

FIGURE 10.15

The pooled OR.

	Disease	No Disease	
Exposed	A	B	Disease Total
Not Exposed	C	D	No Disease Total
	Exposed Total	Not Exposed Total	TOTAL

FIGURE 10.16

The two by two table.

	Author	a	b	c	d
1	AA	10	20	30	40
2	BB	15	12	23	34
3	CC	43	23	35	12
4	DD	8	16	20	28
5	EE	19	29	39	49
6	FF	76	65	54	43
7	GG	20	22	15	12
8	HH	10	20	30	40
9	II	43	23	35	12
10	JJ	8	16	20	28

FIGURE 10.17

The spreadsheet of extracted data.

The spreadsheet of extracted data of included studies will be as follow (Fig. 10.17):

For pooling ORs or RRs, you need to type the following command in the command window:

```
metan a b c d, or label(namevar=Author)
               ↓
               for pooling ORs
```

You will see the following results in the result window (Fig. 10.18):

The pooled OR is estimated as 0.81(95% CI:0.63−1.04), which is not statistically significant as the corresponding CI includes 1. The heterogeneity chi-square

```
. metan a b c d, or

            Study   |    OR    [95% Conf. Interval]    % Weight
--------------------+------------------------------------------------
1                   |  0.667      0.273      1.631         9.05
2                   |  1.848      0.732      4.661         4.96
3                   |  0.641      0.280      1.468        10.75
4                   |  0.700      0.251      1.950         6.71
5                   |  0.823      0.403      1.683        12.55
6                   |  0.931      0.554      1.566        22.25
7                   |  0.727      0.275      1.920         7.22
8                   |  0.667      0.273      1.631         9.05
9                   |  0.641      0.280      1.468        10.75
10                  |  0.700      0.251      1.950         6.71
--------------------+------------------------------------------------
M-H pooled OR       |  0.807      0.626      1.041       100.00
--------------------+------------------------------------------------

  Heterogeneity chi-squared =   4.51 (d.f. = 9) p = 0.875
  I-squared (variation in OR attributable to heterogeneity) =   0.0%

  Test of OR=1 : z=   1.65 p = 0.099
```

FIGURE 10.18

The results of pooling ORs in STATA.

is 4.51 with corresponding *P*-value of .875, and I^2 value is 0%, presenting that there is no heterogeneity between results of the included studies.

The test of OR = 1 shows that the obtained results(OR =0.81) does not reject the null hypothesis (corresponding *P* value of z is .099).

As we did not type random in our command, fixed effects model was applied and the Mantel-Haenszel (M-H) method is used for pooling the ORs.

The forest plot is as follow (Fig. 10.19):

If you want to obtain the pooled RR, you can type rr instead of or in the syntax (Fig. 10.20).

```
metan a b c d, rr label(namevar=Author)
```

The pooled RR is estimated as 0.905(95% CI:0.804−1.019), which is not statistically significant (CI included number 1). The heterogeneity chi-square is 4.50 with corresponding *P*-value of 0.876, and I^2 value is 0%, presenting that there is no heterogeneity between results of the included studies.

The corresponding forest plot is as follow (Fig. 10.21):

In your STATA file, you will see that there are six new columns after obtaining the pooled RR (Fig. 10.22).

To obtain funnel plot, you have to type the following command:

```
metafunnel _ES _selogES
```

To see if publication bias exists or not, you can see the corresponding *P*-value of bias (Egger test) is 0.821 and indicates that there is no evidence of publication bias.

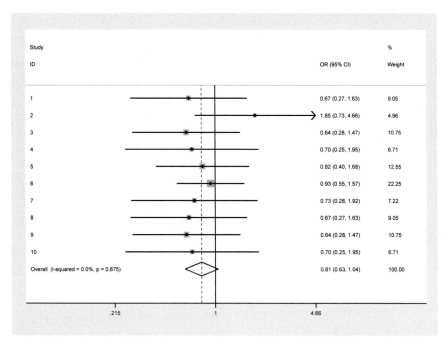

FIGURE 10.19

The forest plot of pooling ORs.

```
. metan a b c d, rr label(namevar=Author)

              Study  |   RR    [95% Conf. Interval]    % Weight
------------------------+------------------------------------------------
AA                   |  0.778     0.438     1.381        6.69
BB                   |  1.377     0.867     2.185        5.50
CC                   |  0.875     0.686     1.116       15.20
DD                   |  0.800     0.415     1.544        4.96
EE                   |  0.893     0.586     1.360       10.23
FF                   |  0.968     0.766     1.224       23.79
GG                   |  0.857     0.539     1.362        6.79
HH                   |  0.778     0.438     1.381        6.69
II                   |  0.875     0.686     1.116       15.20
JJ                   |  0.800     0.415     1.544        4.96
------------------------+------------------------------------------------
M-H pooled RR        |  0.905     0.804     1.019      100.00
------------------------+------------------------------------------------

   Heterogeneity chi-squared =   4.50 (d.f. = 9) p = 0.876
   I-squared (variation in RR attributable to heterogeneity) =   0.0%

   Test of RR=1 : z=   1.65 p = 0.099
```

FIGURE 10.20

Results of pooling RRs.

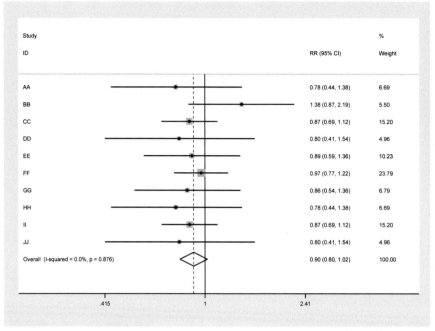

FIGURE 10.21

The forest plot of pooling RRs.

To obtain the results of beg test, you have to type the following command:

```
metabias _ES _selogES, begg
```

To see if publication bias exists or not, you can see the corresponding *P*-value of bias (Begg test) is 0.371, and indicates that there is no evidence of publication bias (Figs 10.23−10.25).

Doing meta-analysis in R software

The other software that is commonly used for meta-analysis is R.

To do your analysis you have to download both R and RStudio.

The preface of RStudio is as follows (Fig. 10.26):

You can import data from STATA to RStudio, Click on 'File,' select 'Import Dataset,' and then choose 'From Stata.(Fig. 10.27):

Now, we are importing our first dataset from STATA to RStudio (data regarding prevalence of RLS in patients with MS) (Fig. 10.28):

To do meta-analysis is R, you have to install the following packages:

1. meta,
2. metafor,
3. dplyr,
4. robumeta.

	Author	a	b	c	d	total1	total2	_SS	_ES	_selogES	_LCI	_UCI	_WT
1	AA	10	20	30	40	30	70	100	.7777778	.29277	.4381767	1.380581	3.906379
2	BB	15	12	23	34	27	57	84	1.376812	.2357202	.8674193	2.185345	6.026065
3	CC	43	23	35	12	66	47	113	.8748918	.1240932	.686003	1.115791	21.7436
4	DD	8	16	20	28	24	48	72	.8	.3354102	.4145609	1.543802	2.976289
5	EE	19	29	39	49	40	88	136	.6931624	.2146524	.5064325	1.360326	7.267018
6	FF	76	65	54	43	141	97	238	.9682164	.1194778	.7660776	1.223692	23.45597
7	GG	20	22	15	12	42	27	69	.8571429	.2362628	.5394435	1.361948	5.998421
8	HH	10	20	30	40	30	70	100	.7777778	.29277	.4381767	1.380581	3.906379
9	II	43	23	35	12	66	47	113	.8748918	.1240932	.686003	1.115791	21.7436
10	JJ	8	16	20	28	24	48	72	.8	.3354102	.4145609	1.543802	2.976289

FIGURE 10.22

The preface of the dataset.

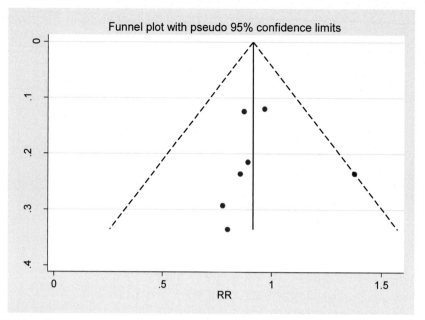

FIGURE 10.23

The funnel plot.

```
Egger's test for small-study effects:
Regress standard normal deviate of intervention
effect estimate against its standard error

Number of studies = 10                          Root MSE    = .7871

      Std_Eff |    Coef.   Std. Err.      t    P>|t|     [95% Conf. Interval]
--------------+------------------------------------------------------------
        slope |  .9406261  .1180029     7.97   0.000     .668511    1.212741
         bias | -.1503537  .6448798    -0.23   0.821   -1.637449    1.336742

Test of H0: no small-study effects          P = 0.821
```

FIGURE 10.24

The results of Egger's test for RRs.

```
Begg's test for small-study effects:
Rank correlation between standardized intervention effect and its standard error

    adj. Kendall's Score (P-Q) =    -10
          Std. Dev. of Score =   11.18 (corrected for ties)
            Number of Studies =      10
                           z =   -0.89
                    Pr > |z| =   0.371
                           z =    0.80 (continuity corrected)
                    Pr > |z| =   0.421 (continuity corrected)
```

FIGURE 10.25

The results of Begg test for pooled RRs.

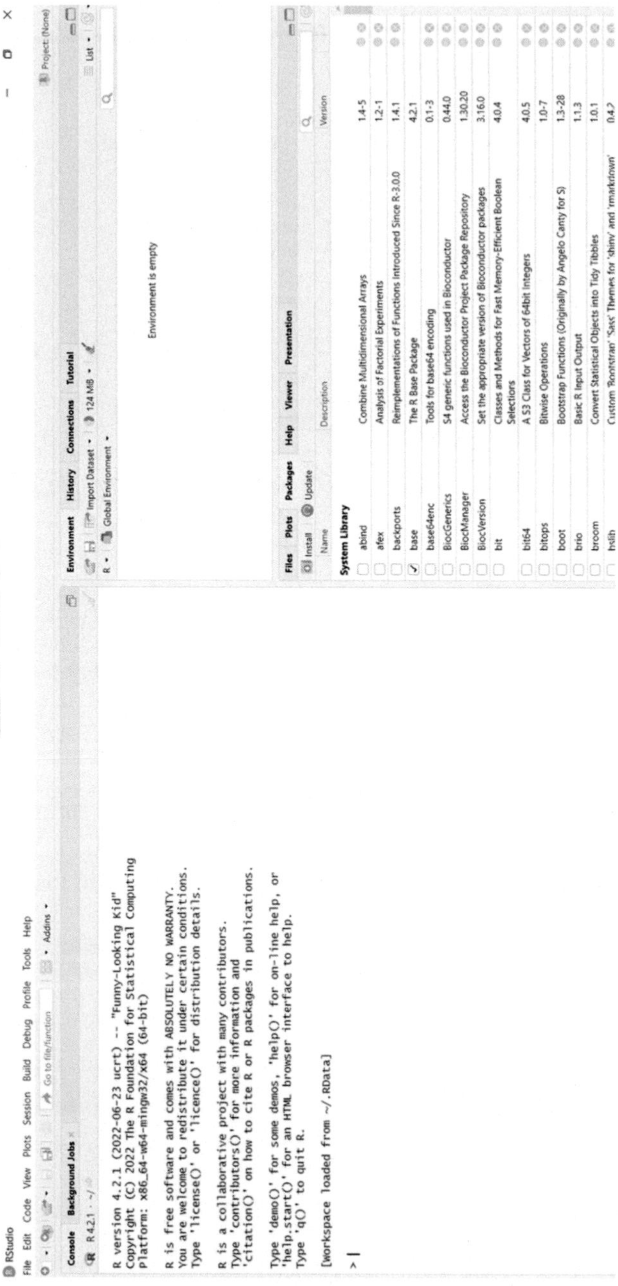

FIGURE 10.26

The preface of RStudio.

FIGURE 10.27

Importing data from other databases to R.

To pool the prevalence of RLS in patients with MS, we have to load the meta package:

Simply use library( ) function.

The commands in RStudio are shown in blue.

The first command is:

```
> library(meta)
```

Then type the following command:

```
>x<-metaprop (RLS,TotalMS,data=Data)
```

and then enter.

```
> x
```

So, you will get the following results (Figs. 10.20 and 10.29):

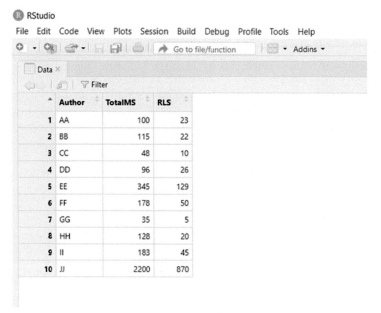

FIGURE 10.28

The preface of data in RSudio.

```
Number of studies combined: k = 10
Number of observations: o = 3428
Number of events: e = 1200

                      proportion            95%-CI
Common effect model      0.3501 [0.3343; 0.3662]
Random effects model     0.2539 [0.2044; 0.3107]

Quantifying heterogeneity:
 tau^2 = 0.1477; tau = 0.3843; I^2 = 89.1% [82.0%; 93.4%]; H = 3.03 [2.36; 3.88]

Test of heterogeneity:
     Q d.f.  p-value              Test
 82.40   9 < 0.0001         wald-type
 93.50   9 < 0.0001 Likelihood-Ratio

Details on meta-analytical method:
- Random intercept logistic regression model
- Maximum-likelihood estimator for tau^2
- Logit transformation
```

FIGURE 10.29

The results of pooling prevalence of RLS in patients with MS.

As you see, the number of studies is reported as 10, and the total number of observations is 3428.

You see the pooled prevalence is calculated by two models:

1. Fixed or common effect models (The pooled prevalence is estimated as 0.3501) and,
2. Random effects method (The pooled prevalence is estimated as 0.2539).

The results regarding heterogeneity between included studies are shown as tauˆ2, Iˆ2, Q, and H test.

When you do meta-analysis in R, you will find H statistics as one of the heterogeneity tests, which describes the relative excess in Q over its degrees of freedom [3].

To obtain forest plot, you have to install forestplot package, and load it:

```
> install.packages("forestplot")
> library(forestplot)
```

To obtain forest plot, type the following command:

```
> forest(x)
```

You will get the following forest plot (Fig. 10.30):

To obtain the pooled SMD (standardized mean difference) of vitamin d level in participants with diabetes and healthy controls, we would import the second dataset into RStudio (Fig. 10.31):

To pool SMDs, the command will be as follows:

```
x<-metacont(N01,mean1,sd1,N02,mean2,sd2,sm="SMD",method.smd="H",
data=Data_2)
```

then you have to enter x:

```
> x
```

In the above command, sm means summary measure, so we choose SMD as we want to pool SMDs, and method.sm is pooling method option that we chose Hedges' g method.

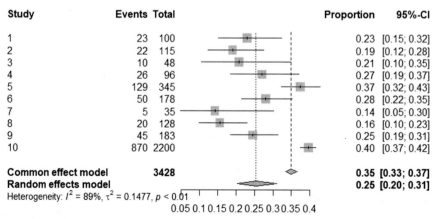

FIGURE 10.30

The forestplot of pooled prevalence of RLS in patients with MS.

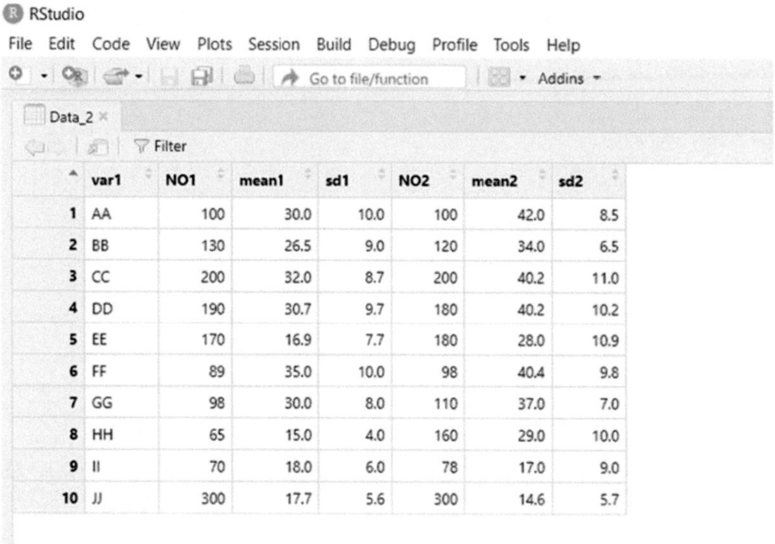

	var1	NO1	mean1	sd1	NO2	mean2	sd2
1	AA	100	30.0	10.0	100	42.0	8.5
2	BB	130	26.5	9.0	120	34.0	6.5
3	CC	200	32.0	8.7	200	40.2	11.0
4	DD	190	30.7	9.7	180	40.2	10.2
5	EE	170	16.9	7.7	180	28.0	10.9
6	FF	89	35.0	10.0	98	40.4	9.8
7	GG	98	30.0	8.0	110	37.0	7.0
8	HH	65	15.0	4.0	160	29.0	10.0
9	II	70	18.0	6.0	78	17.0	9.0
10	JJ	300	17.7	5.6	300	14.6	5.7

FIGURE 10.31

Data view in RStudio.

For pooling SMDs we can use either Cohen's d, or Hedges' g, or Glass' Δ (*delta*) method.

```
Cohen's d= (Mean1-Mean2)/sd pooled
Sd pooled= √[(s12+ s22) / 2]
Hedge's g= (Mean1-Mean2)/sd pooled (Sp)
```

$$S_p = \sqrt{\frac{(n_1-1)s_1^2 + (n_2-1)s_2^2}{(n_2-1)+(n_2-1)}}$$

Glass's delta uses only the control group's standard deviation.

The results will be as follow (Fig. 10.32):

If you want to apply Cohen's d as the method of analysis, you have to type the following command:

```
x<-metacont(NO1,mean1,sd1,NO2,mean2,sd2,sm="SMD",method.smd="C",data
=Data_2)
```

To obtain forest plot (Fig. 10.33)**:**

```
> forest(x)
```

To obtain the funnel plot, you can use the following command (Fig. 10.34):

```
> funnel(x)
```

We will discuss about the funnel plot in Chapter 12.

```
Number of studies combined: k = 10
Number of observations: o = 2938

                        SMD            95%-CI       z  p-value
Common effect model  -0.5953 [-0.6718; -0.5188] -15.25 < 0.0001
Random effects model -0.7548 [-1.1595; -0.3502]  -3.66   0.0003

Quantifying heterogeneity:
 tau^2 = 0.4080 [0.1836; 1.3929]; tau = 0.6387 [0.4285; 1.1802]
 I^2 = 97.2% [96.0%; 98.0%]; H = 5.94 [5.03; 7.01]

Test of heterogeneity:
     Q d.f.  p-value
 317.23   9 < 0.0001

Details on meta-analytical method:
- Inverse variance method
- Restricted maximum-likelihood estimator for tau^2
- Q-Profile method for confidence interval of tau^2 and tau
- Hedges' g (bias corrected standardised mean difference; using exact formulae)
```

FIGURE 10.32

The results of pooling SMDs.

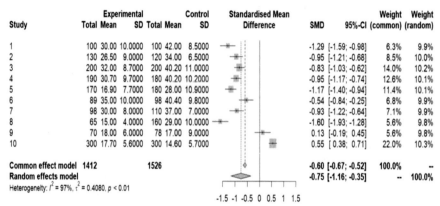

FIGURE 10.33

The forest plot of pooling SMDs.

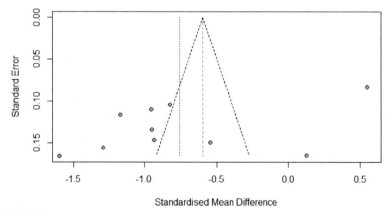

FIGURE 10.34

The funnel plot.

Pooling ORs/RRs in R

To pool ORs or RRs in R, we import our previous data from STAT to R (Fig. 10.35).

In this dataset, column a shows number of events in the exposure group, b shows the number of individuals without event in exposure group, c shows number of events in the control group, and d shows the number of individuals without event in the control group.

First, we have to generate two variables in r.

Total number of people who had exposure:

```
> total1<-a+b
```

And total number of controls (without exposure):

```
> total2<-c+d
```

For pooling ORs, you have to type this command:

```
x<-metabin(data=DATA4,
a,total1,c,total2,random=T,fixed=F,method="Inverse",
sm="OR",studlab=Author)>x
```
then enter x.
```
> x
```

you will see the following results (Fig. 10.36):

Then you can get the forest plot (Fig. 10.37):

```
> forest(x)
```

	Author	a	b	c	d
1	GG	20	22	15	12
2	DD	8	16	20	28
3	JJ	8	16	20	28
4	BB	15	12	23	34
5	AA	10	20	30	40
6	HH	10	20	30	40
7	CC	43	23	35	12
8	II	43	23	35	12
9	EE	19	29	39	49
10	FF	76	65	54	43

DATA_4

FIGURE 10.35

Importing data from STATA to R.

```
Number of studies: k = 10
Number of observations: o = 1097
Number of events: e = 553

                              OR          95%-CI      z p-value
Random effects model 0.8073 [0.6247; 1.0433] -1.64  0.1019

Quantifying heterogeneity:
  tau^2 = 0 [0.0000; 0.1337]; tau = 0 [0.0000; 0.3657]
  I^2 = 0.0% [0.0%; 62.4%]; H = 1.00 [1.00; 1.63]

Test of heterogeneity:
   Q d.f. p-value
 4.51    9  0.8748

Details on meta-analytical method:
 - Inverse variance method
 - Restricted maximum-likelihood estimator for tau^2
 - Q-Profile method for confidence interval of tau^2 and tau
```

FIGURE 10.36

The results of pooling ORs in R.

Study	Experimental Events	Total	Control Events	Total	Odds Ratio	OR	95%-CI	Weight
AA	10	30	30	70		0.67	[0.27; 1.63]	8.2%
BB	15	27	23	57		1.85	[0.73; 4.66]	7.7%
CC	43	66	35	47		0.64	[0.28; 1.47]	9.6%
DD	8	24	20	48		0.70	[0.25; 1.95]	6.3%
EE	19	48	39	88		0.82	[0.40; 1.68]	12.9%
FF	76	141	54	97		0.93	[0.55; 1.57]	24.3%
GG	20	42	15	27		0.73	[0.28; 1.92]	7.0%
HH	10	30	30	70		0.67	[0.27; 1.63]	8.2%
II	43	66	35	47		0.64	[0.28; 1.47]	9.6%
JJ	8	24	20	48		0.70	[0.25; 1.95]	6.3%
Random effects model		498		599		0.81	[0.62; 1.04]	100.0%

Heterogeneity: $I^2 = 0\%$, $\tau^2 = 0$, $p = 0.87$

0.5   1   2

FIGURE 10.37

The forest plot.

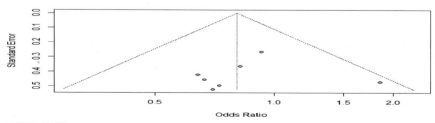

FIGURE 10.38

The funnel plot.

And funnel plot (Fig. 10.38):

```
> funnel(x)
```

To obtain pooled RR, type the following command:

```
x<-metabin(data=DATA_4,a,total1,c,total2,random=T,fixed=
F,method="Inverse",sm="RR",studlab=Author)
```

then enter x:

```
> x
```

The results will be (Fig. 10.39):

To get the forest plot (Fig. 10.40):

```
> forest(x)
```

To obtain funnel plot (Fig. 10.41):

```
> funnel(x)
```

```
Number of studies: k = 10
Number of observations: o = 1097
Number of events: e = 553

                           RR          95%-CI      z p-value
Random effects model  0.9077 [0.8104; 1.0167] -1.67  0.0943

Quantifying heterogeneity:
 tau^2 = 0 [0.0000; 0.0351]; tau = 0 [0.0000; 0.1872]
 I^2 = 0.0% [0.0%; 62.4%]; H = 1.00 [1.00; 1.63]

Test of heterogeneity:
    Q d.f. p-value
 4.50    9  0.8758

Details on meta-analytical method:
- Inverse variance method
- Restricted maximum-likelihood estimator for tau^2
- Q-Profile method for confidence interval of tau^2 and tau
```

FIGURE 10.39

Pooling RRs.

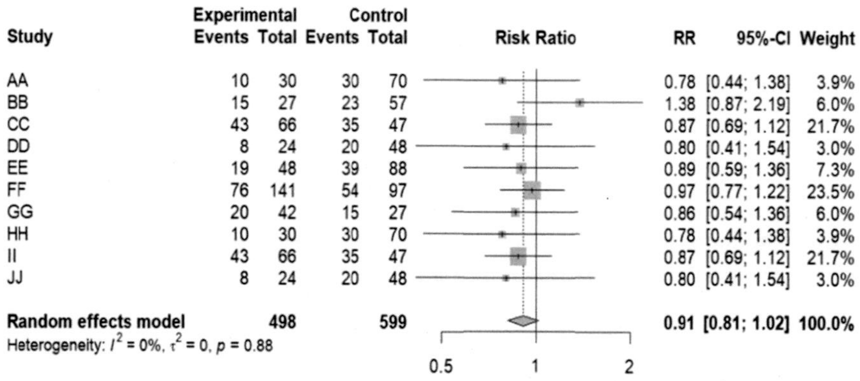

Study	Experimental Events Total		Control Events Total		Risk Ratio	RR	95%-CI	Weight
AA	10	30	30	70		0.78	[0.44; 1.38]	3.9%
BB	15	27	23	57		1.38	[0.87; 2.19]	6.0%
CC	43	66	35	47		0.87	[0.69; 1.12]	21.7%
DD	8	24	20	48		0.80	[0.41; 1.54]	3.0%
EE	19	48	39	88		0.89	[0.59; 1.36]	7.3%
FF	76	141	54	97		0.97	[0.77; 1.22]	23.5%
GG	20	42	15	27		0.86	[0.54; 1.36]	6.0%
HH	10	30	30	70		0.78	[0.44; 1.38]	3.9%
II	43	66	35	47		0.87	[0.69; 1.12]	21.7%
JJ	8	24	20	48		0.80	[0.41; 1.54]	3.0%
Random effects model		498		599		0.91	[0.81; 1.02]	100.0%

Heterogeneity: $I^2 = 0\%$, $\tau^2 = 0$, $p = 0.88$

0.5   1   2

FIGURE 10.40

The forest plot.

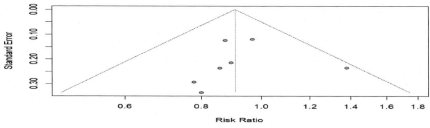

FIGURE 10.41

The funnel plot.

	Author	OR	LL	UL
1	AA	2.10	1.3	4.0
2	BB	1.89	0.9	6.4
3	CC	2.00	0.9	3.1
4	DD	1.70	1.3	3.2
5	EE	0.80	0.6	2.5
6	FF	3.70	2.0	4.3
7	GG	4.20	3.1	6.8
8	HH	1.90	1.1	4.0
9	II	0.70	0.6	1.7
10	JJ	2.90	1.8	4.0

FIGURE 10.42

The spreadsheet of data.

Pooling ORs/RRs when we have crude values:

To pool ORs, when we have ORs, and corresponding CIs, we will import our previous data (Fig. 10.42).

Then we have to generate natural logarithms of OR, LL, and UL.

```
> lnor<-log(OR)
> lnll<-log(LL)
> lnul<-log(UL)
```

Log command in R is used to obtain natural logarithm (ln) values.

Then we have to generate standard error of logarithmic value of OR (lnor).

```
SeLogOR= (ln (Upper limit of CI) − (ln of Lower limit of CI)) / 4
```

The command in r would be:

```
se<-((lnul-lnll)/4)
```

```
> x

Fixed-Effects Model (k = 10)

I^2 (total heterogeneity / total variability):   81.68%
H^2 (total variability / sampling variability):  5.46

Test for Heterogeneity:
Q(df = 9) = 49.1364, p-val < .0001

Model Results:

estimate      se     zval    pval    ci.lb   ci.ub
  0.8160  0.0797  10.2426  <.0001  0.6599  0.9722  ***

---
Signif. codes:  0 '***' 0.001 '**' 0.01 '*' 0.05 '.' 0.1 ' ' 1
```

FIGURE 10.43

Results of pooling ORs in R.

Now, to pool ORs, we have to type this command:

```
> x<-rma(yi=lnor, sei=se, method="FE", measure="OR", data=DATA_3)
```

(FE means fixed effect model) After entering x, we will get the following results (Fig. 10.43):

To obtain forest plot, please type the following command (Fig. 10.44):

```
> forest(x)
```

To obtain funnel plot, please type the following command (Fig. 10.45):

```
> funnel(x)
```

If you have RRs, you can replace OR with RR in the command:

```
> x<-rma(yi=lnor, sei=se, method="FE", measure="RR", data=DATA_3)
```

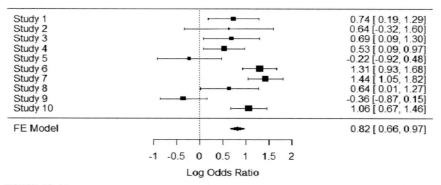

FIGURE 10.44

The forest plot.

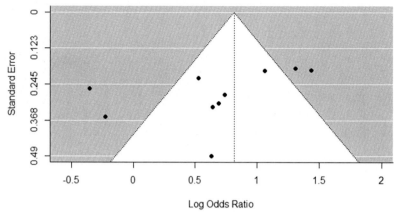

FIGURE 10.45

Funnel plot.

FIGURE 10.46

The preface of RevMan.

Meta-analysis using RevMan

One of the most commonly used softwares for meta-analysis of clinical trials is Rev-Man, which is Cochrane's adapted software [4].

To start analyzing with RevMan, download the software, and then open it (Fig. 10.46):

Click on File, click on New, then you will see the RevMan wizard (Fig. 10.47):

By clicking on next, you will see new review wizard (Fig. 10.48):

Choose intervention review, click on next, then you can name your review (I changed the name to vitamin d) (Fig. 10.49):

Then click on next, and choose Full review (Fig. 10.50):

FIGURE 10.47

Get new review wizard.

FIGURE 10.48

New review wizard.

FIGURE 10.49

Changing the name of the review.

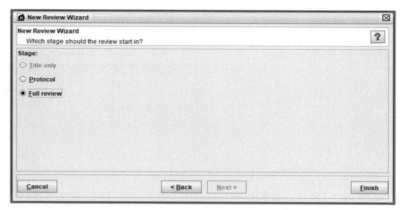

FIGURE 10.50

RevMan review wizard.

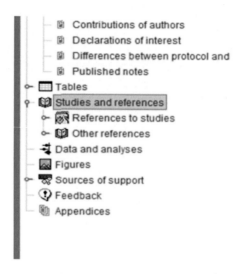

FIGURE 10.51

Studies and references.

By clicking on Finish, you will return to the main page of RevMan, then click on. Studies and references (Fig. 10.51):

Click on References to studies, and then right click on included studies, to add studies (Fig. 10.52):

Click on Add study, enter study ID, click on next, then next, then add publication year,

Click 'Next', then click 'Next' again, and select 'Add Another Study' in the same section (Fig. 10.53):

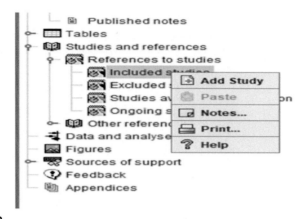

FIGURE 10.52

Adding studies to RevMan.

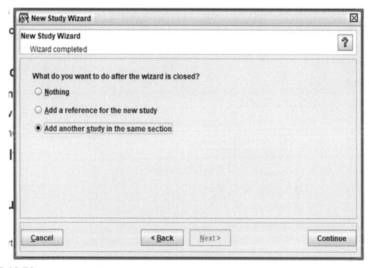

FIGURE 10.53

Adding more studies to RevMan.

I entered all study IDs for vitamin d and MS dataset. If I click on included studies, I can see all study IDs (Fig. 10.54):

You can right click on Data and analyses, to add comparisons (Fig. 10.55):

After clicking on Add Comparison, you have to enter the name of your comparison wizard (I named it Vitamin D) (Fig. 10.56):

Click on next, and select **Add an outcome under the new comparison**, then click on next and now select dichotomous (Fig. 10.57):

FIGURE 10.54

The preface IDs of included studies.

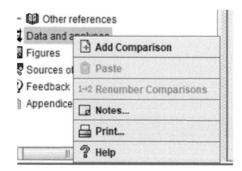

FIGURE 10.55

Adding data in RevMan.

Then click on Finish.

Now, under Data and analyses, you can see your Vitamin D review (Fig. 10.58):

Then right click on Vitamin D, select dichotomous, then click on next, then again next, and you will see following options for your meta-analysis (Fig. 10.59):

I do not change the options, then click on next, so you will see other options for confidence intervals and totals (Fig. 10.60):

FIGURE 10.56

Naming the RevMan wizard.

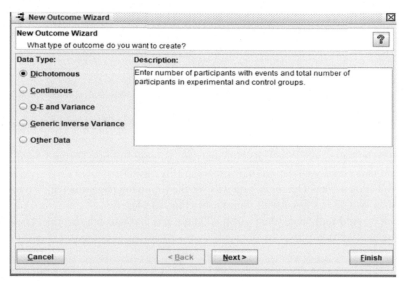

FIGURE 10.57

Adding additional data in RevMan.

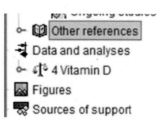

FIGURE 10.58

Data created for meta-analysis.

FIGURE 10.59

The options for dichotomous data meta-analysis.

If you click on next, you can see left and right graph label, scale, and sorting options (Fig. 10.61):

Click on next, the default option is Edit the new outcome, so do not change it (Fig. 10.62):

On the left side, under the Data and analyses, you see Vitamin D comparison option, and under that you can see new outcome (Fig. 10.63):

If you click on new Outcome, you will see the following page, then click on Add study data (which is shown with pink flash) (Fig. 10.64):

Click on Add study data, then select all study IDs that you entered, then click on Finish (Fig. 10.65).

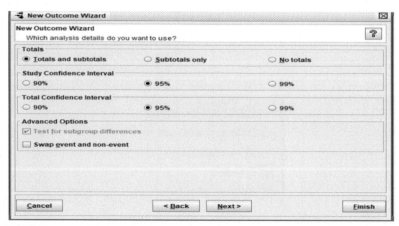

FIGURE 10.60

The options for new outcome wizard.

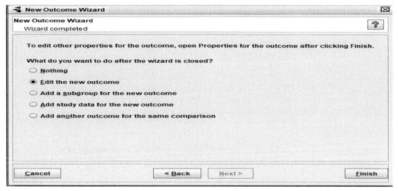

FIGURE 10.61

Options for outcome wizard.

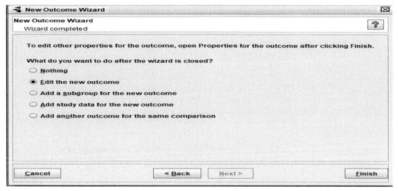

FIGURE 10.62

Outcome wizard in RevMan.

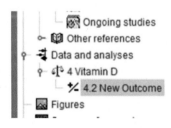

FIGURE 10.63

Viewing data wizard.

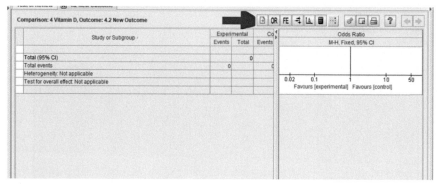

FIGURE 10.64

The wizard view in RevMan.

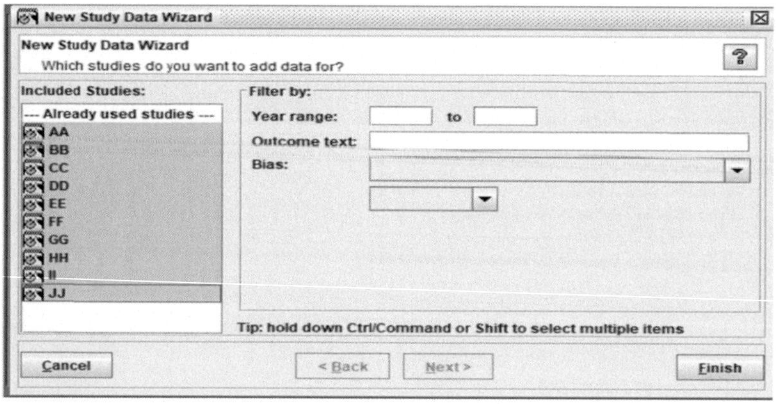

FIGURE 10.65

Adding study data.

You will see the following picture (Fig. 10.66):

Then you can copy and paste the data to the columns (please consider that unlike STATA or R, you have to enter total number of experimental group and controls for both RR and OR calculation). As you can see, the pooled OR is 0.81(95% CI: 0.63–1.04) (Fig. 10.67).

If you click on OR icon (which is circled by red in Fig. 10.58), you will get pooled RR or RD (risk difference) (Fig. 10.68):

You can choose fixed effect model by clicking on RE icon, and you can get forest plot by clicking on forest plot icon next to RE (Fig. 10.69).

If you want to calculate standardized mean difference (SMD) in RevMan, you can go through the steps we described in details before, add study IDs, then right click on Data and analyses, then Add Comparison. Name comparison as Vitamin D mean, click on next, select Add an outcome under the new comparison, then click

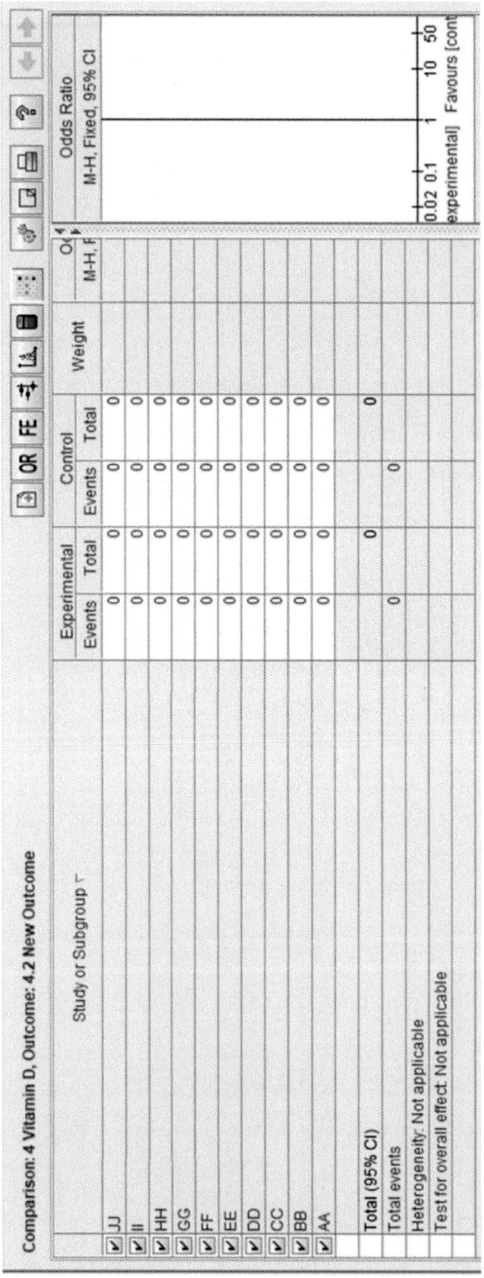

FIGURE 10.66

The data view wizard.

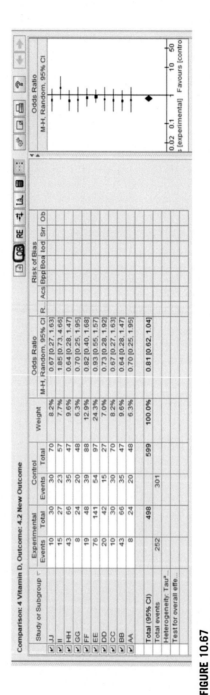

Comparison: 4 Vitamin D, Outcome: 4.2 New Outcome

Study or Subgroup	Experimental Events	Experimental Total	Control Events	Control Total	Weight	Odds Ratio M-H, Random, 95% CI
JJ	10	30	30	70	8.2%	0.67 [0.27, 1.63]
II	15	27	23	57	7.7%	1.85 [0.73, 4.66]
HH	43	66	35	47	9.6%	0.64 [0.28, 1.47]
GG	8	24	20	48	6.3%	0.70 [0.25, 1.95]
FF	19	48	39	88	12.9%	0.82 [0.40, 1.68]
EE	76	141	54	97	24.3%	0.93 [0.55, 1.57]
DD	20	42	15	27	7.0%	0.73 [0.28, 1.92]
CC	10	30	30	70	8.2%	0.67 [0.27, 1.63]
BB	43	66	35	47	9.6%	0.64 [0.28, 1.47]
AA	8	24	20	48	6.3%	0.70 [0.25, 1.95]
Total (95% CI)		498		599	100.0%	0.81 [0.62, 1.04]
Total events	252		301			
Heterogeneity: Tau²...						
Test for overall effe...						

FIGURE 10.67

The pooled OR results.

| Text of Review | ☒ 4.2 New Outcome |

Comparison: 4 Vitamin D, Outcome: 4.2 New Outcome

Study or Subgroup	Experimental		Control		Weight	Risk Ratio M-H, Random, 95% CI	Risk of Bias R... Acs Bpp Boa Iod Srr Ob
	Events	Total	Events	Total			
JJ	10	30	30	70	3.9%	0.78 [0.44, 1.38]	
II	15	27	23	57	6.0%	1.38 [0.87, 2.19]	
HH	43	66	35	47	21.7%	0.87 [0.69, 1.12]	
GG	8	24	20	48	3.0%	0.80 [0.41, 1.54]	
FF	19	48	39	88	7.3%	0.89 [0.59, 1.36]	
EE	76	141	54	97	23.5%	0.97 [0.77, 1.22]	
DD	20	42	15	27	6.0%	0.86 [0.54, 1.36]	
CC	10	30	30	70	3.9%	0.78 [0.44, 1.38]	
BB	43	66	35	47	21.7%	0.87 [0.69, 1.12]	
AA	8	24	20	48	3.0%	0.80 [0.41, 1.54]	
Total (95% CI)		498		599	100.0%	0.91 [0.81, 1.02]	
Total events	252		301				
Heterogeneity: Tau²...							
Test for overall effe...							

FIGURE 10.68

The pooled RR.

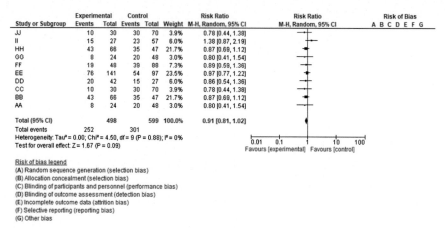

Study or Subgroup	Experimental Events	Total	Control Events	Total	Weight	Risk Ratio M-H, Random, 95% CI
JJ	10	30	30	70	3.9%	0.78 [0.44, 1.38]
II	15	27	23	57	6.0%	1.38 [0.87, 2.19]
HH	43	66	35	47	21.7%	0.87 [0.69, 1.12]
GG	8	24	20	48	3.0%	0.80 [0.41, 1.54]
FF	19	48	39	88	7.3%	0.89 [0.59, 1.36]
EE	76	141	54	97	23.5%	0.97 [0.77, 1.22]
DD	20	42	15	27	6.0%	0.86 [0.54, 1.36]
CC	10	30	30	70	3.9%	0.78 [0.44, 1.38]
BB	43	66	35	47	21.7%	0.87 [0.69, 1.12]
AA	8	24	20	48	3.0%	0.80 [0.41, 1.54]
Total (95% CI)		498		599	100.0%	0.91 [0.81, 1.02]
Total events	252		301			

Heterogeneity: Tau² = 0.00; Chi² = 4.50, df = 9 (P = 0.88); I² = 0%
Test for overall effect: Z = 1.67 (P = 0.09)

Risk of bias legend
(A) Random sequence generation (selection bias)
(B) Allocation concealment (selection bias)
(C) Blinding of participants and personnel (performance bias)
(D) Blinding of outcome assessment (detection bias)
(E) Incomplete outcome data (attrition bias)
(F) Selective reporting (reporting bias)
(G) Other bias

FIGURE 10.69

Forest plot.

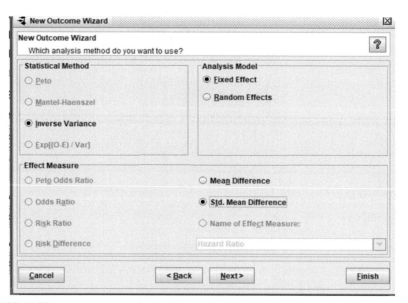

FIGURE 10.70

The outcome wizard.

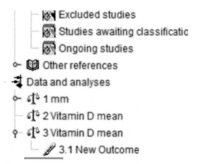

FIGURE 10.71

The new outcome list.

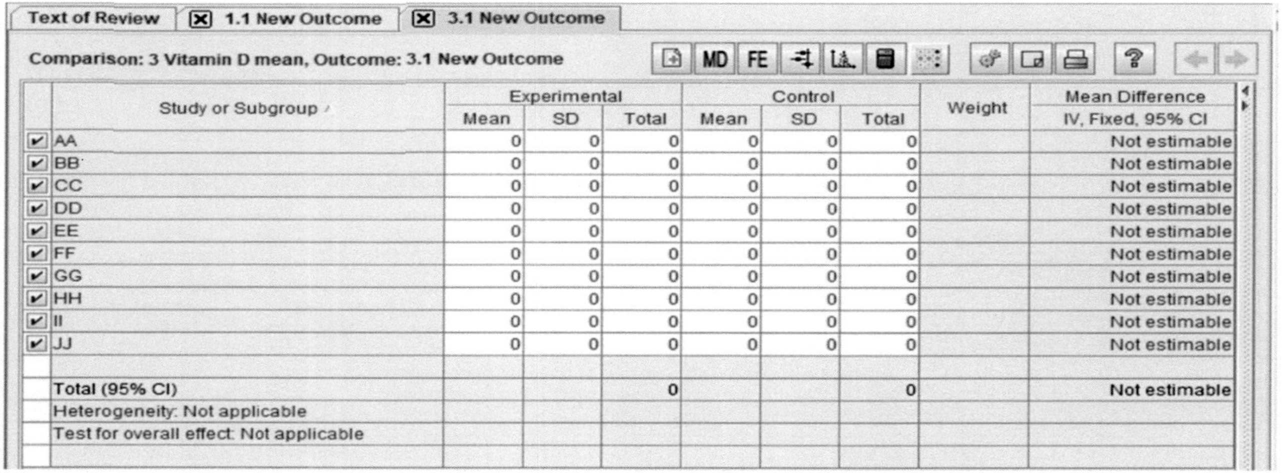

FIGURE 10.72

New outcome wizard.

Study or Subgroup	Experimental			Control			Weight	Std. Mean Difference IV, Random, 95% CI
	Mean	SD	Total	Mean	SD	Total		
AA	30	10	100	42	8.5	100	9.9%	-1.29 [-1.59, -0.98]
BB	26.5	9	130	34	6.5	120	10.0%	-0.95 [-1.21, -0.68]
CC	32	8.7	200	40.2	11	200	10.1%	-0.83 [-1.03, -0.62]
DD	30.7	9.7	190	40.2	10.2	180	10.1%	-0.95 [-1.17, -0.74]
EE	16.9	7.7	170	28	10.9	180	10.1%	-1.17 [-1.40, -0.94]
FF	35	10	89	40.4	9.8	98	9.9%	-0.54 [-0.84, -0.25]
GG	30	8	98	37	7	110	9.9%	-0.93 [-1.22, -0.64]
HH	15	4	65	29	10	160	9.8%	-1.60 [-1.93, -1.28]
II	18	6	70	17	9	78	9.8%	0.13 [-0.19, 0.45]
JJ	17.7	5.6	300	14.6	5.7	300	10.2%	0.55 [0.38, 0.71]
Total (95% CI)			1412			1526	100.0%	-0.76 [-1.22, -0.29]
Heterogeneity: Tau² = 0.54; Chi² = 317.21, df = 9 (P < 0.00001); I² = 97%								
Test for overall effect: Z = 3.21 (P = 0.001)								

FIGURE 10.73

The pooled SMD result in RevMan.

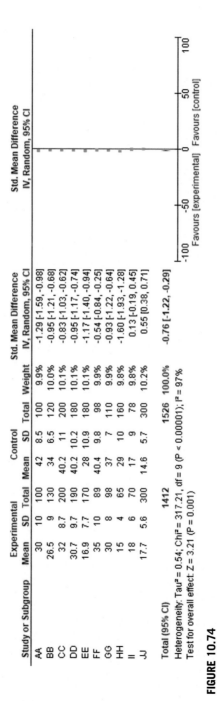

| Study or Subgroup | Experimental | | | Control | | | | | Std. Mean Difference | Std. Mean Difference |
	Mean	SD	Total	Mean	SD	Total	Weight	IV, Random, 95% CI	IV, Random, 95% CI
AA	30	10	100	42	8.5	100	9.9%	-1.29 [-1.59, -0.98]	
BB	26.5	9	130	34	6.5	120	10.0%	-0.95 [-1.21, -0.68]	
CC	32	8.7	200	40.2	11	200	10.1%	-0.83 [-1.03, -0.62]	
DD	30.7	9.7	190	40.2	10.2	180	10.1%	-0.95 [-1.17, -0.74]	
EE	16.9	7.7	170	28	10.9	180	10.1%	-1.17 [-1.40, -0.94]	
FF	35	10	89	40.4	9.8	98	9.9%	-0.54 [-0.84, -0.25]	
GG	30	8	98	37	7	110	9.9%	-0.93 [-1.22, -0.64]	
HH	15	4	65	29	10	160	9.8%	-1.60 [-1.93, -1.28]	
II	18	6	70	17	9	78	9.8%	0.13 [-0.19, 0.45]	
JJ	17.7	5.6	300	14.6	5.7	300	10.2%	0.55 [0.38, 0.71]	
Total (95% CI)			1412			1526	100.0%	-0.76 [-1.22, -0.29]	

Heterogeneity: Tau² = 0.54; Chi² = 317.21, df = 9 (P < 0.00001); I² = 97%
Test for overall effect: Z = 3.21 (P = 0.001)

FIGURE 10.74

Forest plot of SMD in RevMan.

continue and select continuous. Click on next, again click on next, then you will see the following image (Fig. 10.70):

I selected standardized mean difference (Std. Mean Difference) instead of Mean Difference.

You will have new outcome under Vitamin D mean on the left side (Fig. 10.71):

Right click on New Outcome, click on Add study data, select all study IDs (control A), then click on Finish. You will see the following picture (Fig. 10.72):

Then copy and paste data on RevMan, you will get the following results (Fig. 10.73):

By clicking on forest plot, you will get the following plot (Fig. 10.74):

Meta-analysis using SPSS (statistical package for the social sciences)

SPSS is commonly used software for data-analysis. From version 26, SPSS has meta-analysis option. To start meta-analysis using SPSS, go to Analyze, you can see meta-analysis option in the menu (Fig. 10.75).

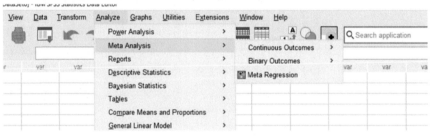

FIGURE 10.75

The meta-analysis menu.

	var1	NO 1	mean 1	sd1	NO 2	mean 2	sd2
1	AA	100	30.00	10.00	100	42.00	8.50
2	BB	130	26.50	9.00	120	34.00	6.50
3	CC	200	32.00	8.70	200	40.20	11.00
4	DD	190	30.70	9.70	180	40.20	10.20
5	EE	170	16.90	7.70	180	28.00	10.90
6	FF	89	35.00	10.00	98	40.40	9.80
7	GG	98	30.00	8.00	110	37.00	7.00
8	HH	65	15.00	4.00	160	29.00	10.00
9	II	70	18.00	6.00	78	17.00	9.00
10	JJ	300	17.70	5.60	300	14.60	5.70

FIGURE 10.76

Preface of data in SPSS.

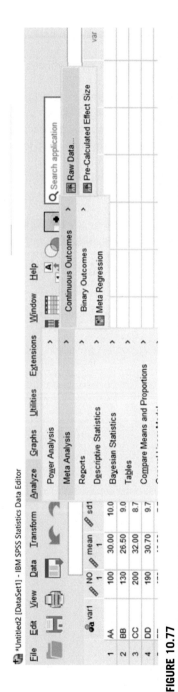

FIGURE 10.77

How to start meta-analysis of continuous data.

When you click on meta-analysis, you can choose between continuous outcomes, Binary outcomes or Meta Regression.

If we open our second database (for SMD) here, we can see this preface (Fig. 10.76):

For meta-analysis, from Analyze menu, select meta-analysis, and then click on continuous Outcomes, then Raw Data (Fig. 10.77).

Click on Raw Data, and move items to the right places. You can choose the method for pooling SMDs (Figs. 10.78 and 10.79):

To obtain forestplot, click on plot option, select Effect size, Confidence interval limit, and weight. You can also select heterogeneity and test to get heterogeneity results (Fig. 10.80):

To obtain funnel plot, you can select funnel from plot option, and for label you can select the name of the studies (Fig. 10.81):

The funnel plot will be as follows (Fig. 10.82):

To assess publication bias, from the menu on your right, select bias (Fig. 10.83):

Then select egger-regression-based test, and click on continue (Fig. 10.84):

The results will be as follows (Fig. 10.85):

The corresponding P-value of egger test is 0.277, indicating no evidence of publication bias.

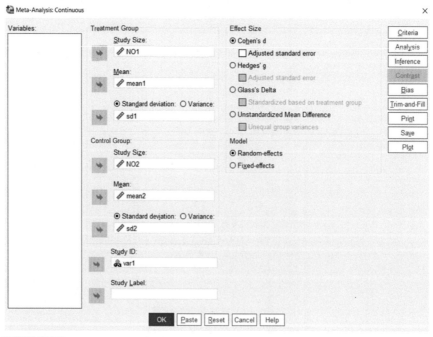

FIGURE 10.78

The preface of continuous data meta-analysis.

➡ **Meta-Analysis: Continuous Outcomes with Raw Data**

Meta-Analysis Summary

Data Type	Raw
Outcome Type	Continuous
Effect Size Measure	Cohen's d
Model	Random-effects
Weight	Inverse-variance[a]
Estimation Method	REML
Standard Error Adjustment	None

a. Random-effects weights including both within-
and between-study variance.

**Case Processing
Summary**

	N	Percent
Included	10	100.0%
Missing	0	0.0%
Invalid[a]	0	0.0%
Total	10	100.0%

a. Nonpositive variance or
standard error, or
insufficient study size.

Effect Size Estimates

	Effect Size	Std. Error	Z	Sig. (2-tailed)	95% Confidence Interval Lower	95% Confidence Interval Upper
Overall	-.757	.2070	-3.658	<.001	-1.163	-.351

FIGURE 10.79

The meta-analysis results.

For binary outcomes, if we have OR, and standard error of OR (se), the meta-analysis will be simple.

Click on Analyze, click on meta-analysis, then choose binary outcomes, click on precalculated effect size, and move OR to the effect size and **se** to Standard Error, select the study ID, and then select forest plot from plot section (**select effect size, confidence interval, and exponential form**) (Fig. 10.86).

The results will be as follows (Fig. 10.87):

To get heterogeneity results, you can choose heterogeneity and test from Annotation section in the Plot option (Fig. 10.88):

The forest plot will be as follow (Fig. 10.89):

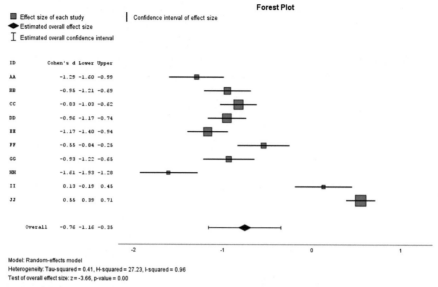

FIGURE 10.80

The forest plot.

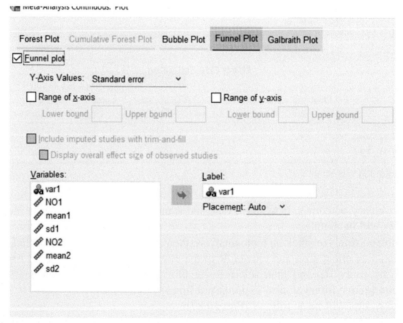

FIGURE 10.81

Getting funnel plot.

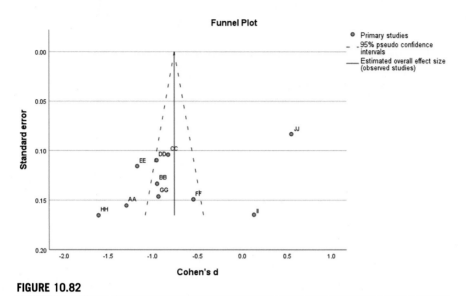

FIGURE 10.82

The funnel plot.

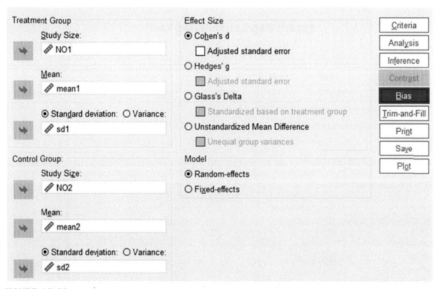

FIGURE 10.83

Selecting the bias option.

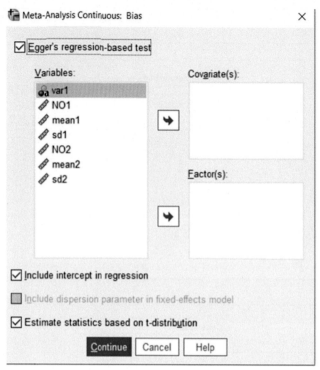

FIGURE 10.84

Selecting Egger test.

Egger's Regression-Based Test[a]

Parameter	Coefficient	Std. Error	t	Sig. (2-tailed)	95% Confidence Interval Lower	Upper
(Intercept)	.407	1.0191	.399	.700	-1.943	2.757
SE[b]	-8.799	7.5492	-1.166	.277	-26.207	8.610

a. Random-effects meta-regression

b. Standard error of effect size

FIGURE 10.85

The results of Egger test.

FIGURE 10.86

Meta-analysis of binary outcomes in SPSS.

Meta-Analysis Summary

Data Type	Pre-calculated
Outcome Type	Binary
Effect Size Measure	@OR
Model	Random-effects
Weight	Inverse-variance[a]
Estimation Method	REML
Standard Error Adjustment	None

a. Random-effects weights including both within- and between-study variance.

Case Processing Summary

	N	Percent
Included	10	100.0%
Missing	0	0.0%
Invalid[a]	0	0.0%
Dropped[b]	0	0.0%
Total	10	100.0%

a. Nonpositive variance or standard error.

b. Studies with either no success cases or no failure cases.

Effect Size Estimates

	Effect Size	Std. Error	Z	Sig. (2-tailed)	95% Confidence Interval Lower	95% Confidence Interval Upper
Overall	2.093	.3681	5.686	<.001	1.371	2.814

FIGURE 10.87

The results of meta-analysis in SPSS.

To obtain pooled OR using the raw data, open the forth database in SPSS (which provide a b c d data for calculating OR or RR) click on Analyze menu, meta-analysis, Binary Outcomes, Raw Data, then move items to the correct windows (Fig. 10.90):

For OR and RR, please select display exponential form, so the proper pooled OR or RR will be displayed at the bottom of the forest plot (Fig. 10.91):

And if you select RR, the forest plot will be as follow (Fig. 10.92):

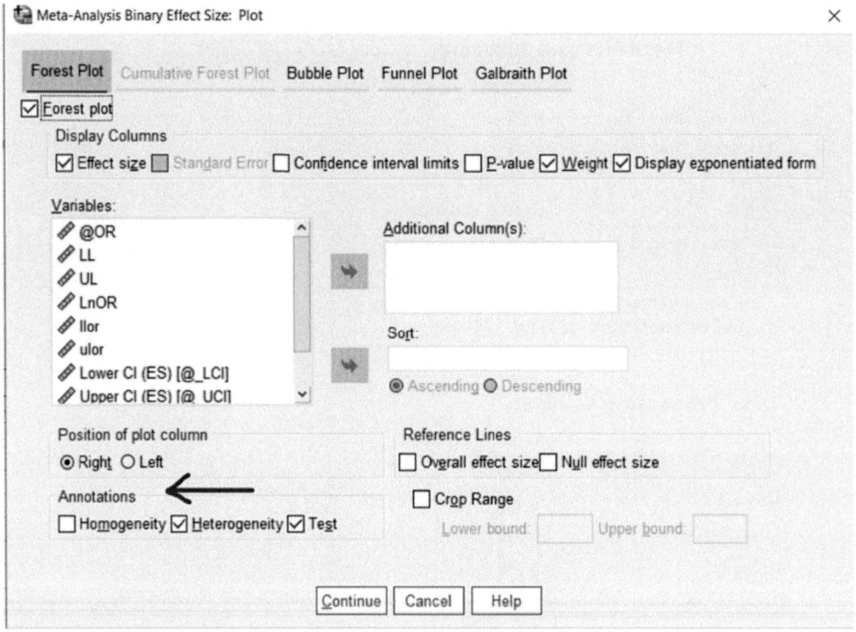

FIGURE 10.88

Selecting heterogeneity tests.

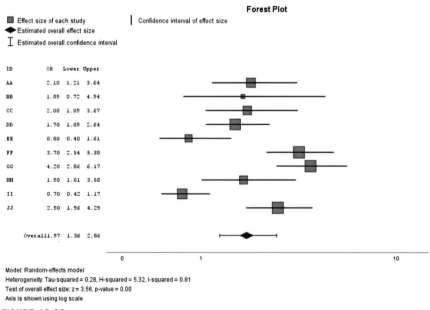

FIGURE 10.89

The forest plot.

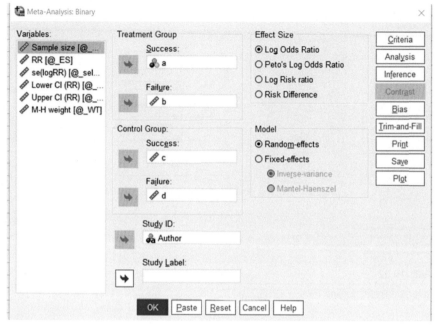

FIGURE 10.90

Doing meta-analysis in SPSS.

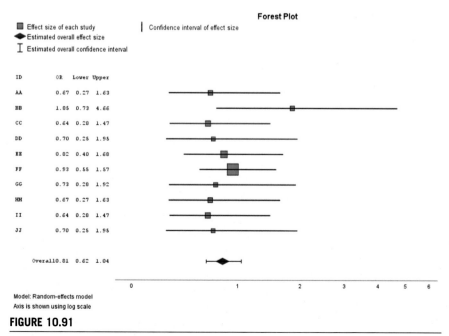

FIGURE 10.91

The forest plot of pooling ORs in SPSS.

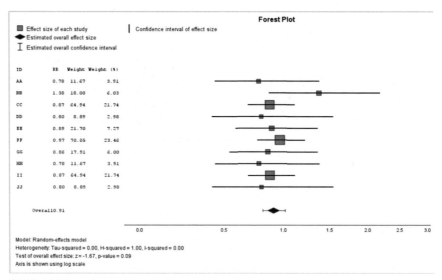

FIGURE 10.92

The forest plot of pooling RRs in SPSS.

References

[1] https://www.drandyteh.com/stata/install-meta-analysis-commands-in-stata-metan-metafunnel/.

[2] Andrade C. How to use percentiles to better understand standardized mean difference (SMD) as a measure of effect size. J Clin Psychiatry 2023;84(4):48350.

[3] Higgins JP, Thompson SG. Quantifying heterogeneity in a meta-analysis. Stat Med 2002; 21(11):1539—58.

[4] https://training.cochrane.org/online-learning/core-software/revman.

Interpretation of results in the forest plot

11

Mahsa Ghajarzadeh

Department of Neurology, Johns Hopkins University School of Medicine, Baltimore, MD, United States

What is a forest plot?

A forest plot is commonly used in systematic reviews that include meta-analyses. It visually presents the results of individual studies included in the meta-analysis, along with the overall pooled estimate of effect sizes, providing a clear summary of the data. It provides the point estimate with confidence interval for each included study, the pooled estimate with its confidence interval, the no effect line (null line), and the proportionate weight of each study contributed to the meta-analysis.

It also provides visual picture of the quantity of variation between the results of the included studies [1]. It's name originates from the idea that the plot seems like a forest of lines and was names after Pat Forrest (breast cancer researcher) in September 1990, at the meeting of the breast cancer overview [1].

For the first time, forest plots were introduced in 1970s by Freiman et al. [2] by displaying the results of individual studies with horizontal lines and a mark for the point estimate. The horizontal line represents the confidence interval of the point estimate, and the squares centered on the confidence interval of each study show the point estimate of each study.

The area of each square reflects the weight that the individual study contributed to the meta-analysis [1]. If the sample size of the study is large, it provides more information and gets higher weight in the pooled analysis [3].

Each forest plot has a vertical "no effect line," which equals to one for binary outcomes and zero for continuous outcomes.

If the horizontal line (confidence interval of each study or the CI of the pooled estimate) crosses the no effect line, it means that there was no significant difference between compared groups for continuous variables or no association for binary outcomes.

The diamond at the bottom of the figure represents the information regarding the pooled estimate.

The center of the diamond at the bottom shows the pooled estimate, and the width of the diamond represents the confidence interval of the pooled estimate.

Systematic Review and Meta-Analysis. https://doi.org/10.1016/B978-0-443-13428-9.00011-2

The eyeballing approach allows you to evaluate if the included studies are estimating the same thing or not. When estimates vary widely and confidence intervals do not overlap, it may suggest variability between the results of the studies.

The forest plots which are obtained by STATA or R show only I^2 (I-squared statistic) for heterogeneity, while the forest plots, which are obtained by RevMan provide all heterogeneity indexes such as Tau^2, I^2, and Chi square (Figs. 11.1–11.3).

As you can see in Fig. 11.1, the first column of the figure shows the name of the authors using label option as we obtained in our STATA command.

The point estimate of each study is shown as a square, and the confidence interval of each study is presented by horizontal line including the point estimate.

For instance, for the first study, the point estimate of SMD IS -1.29 with 95% CI as −1.6, −0.99, and weight percent as 9.89%.

In this figure, the percent of weights of included studies is close to each other, so the area of the squares is not very different. The confidence interval of the study II (above study JJ) crosses the no effect line, and the confidence interval (−0.19, 0.45) includes zero, showing no significant difference between SMDs of two groups in study II.

The overall I^2 is estimated as 97.2%, and the corresponding P value is less than 0.001, which shows significant variability between the results of the included studies.

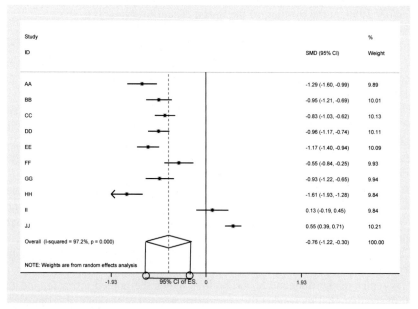

FIGURE 11.1

The forest plot of pooled standardized mean difference (SMD) which is made by STATA.

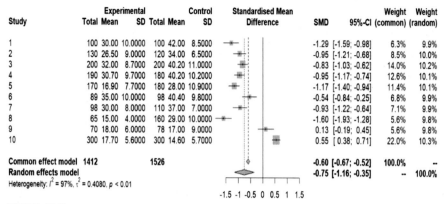

FIGURE 11.2

The forest plot of pooled standardized mean difference (SMD), which is made by R.

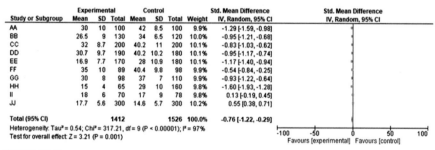

FIGURE 11.3

The forest plot obtained, which is made by RevMan.

As you can see, the weights are obtained using the random effects model, and the pooled SMD is estimated as −0.76, which is shown by the dashed red line.

The 95% CI of the pooled estimate is shown as the larger diameter of the diamond (−1.22, −0.3).

Under the SMD column (effect size column), you can see the SMD of each study and corresponding confidence interval, and the last column shows the percent of weight that each study contributes in the meta-analysis.

Fig. 11.2 provides mean and standard deviation (SD) of each group in respectively included study as well as the corresponding weight of each study based on the random and common (fixed) effects models.

You can also see I^2 (97%) as well as T^2 (0.4080) and heterogeneity related P value (<0.01).

The figure provides two diamonds, the first small one corresponds to the pooled estimate using common (fixed) effects model, and the larger one corresponds to the pooled estimate using random effects model.

Fig. 11.3 which is obtained in RevMan provides information regarding study ID, mean, and SD, as well as standardized mean difference (SMD) of each study obtained by inverse variance (IV) method of random effects model.

Heterogeneity results as well as test of overall effect are also provided ($Z = 3.21$, $P = .001$).

In general, the forest plot provides information regarding point estimate and corresponding confidence interval of each individual study, the pooled estimate, and its confidence interval, the null line of the effect size, corresponding weight of each study, the overlap of the confidence intervals, and the statistical heterogeneity.

References

[1] Lewis S, Clarke M. Forest plots: trying to see the wood and the trees. BMJ 2001; 322(7300):1479—80.
[2] Ja F. The importance of beta, the type II error and sample size in the design and interpretation of the randomized control trial. Survey of 71" negative" trials. N Engl J Med 1978; 299:690—4.
[3] Dettori JR, Norvell DC, Chapman JR. Seeing the forest by looking at the trees: how to interpret a meta-analysis forest plot. Global Spine J 2021;11(4):614—6.

Publication bias and funnel plot

12

Masoumeh Sadeghi

Department of Epidemiology, School of Health, Mashhad University of Medical Sciences, Mashhad, Iran

Introduction

Publication bias is one of the main threats of meta-analyses

Meta-analysis provides valuable results on the effect size of the studies. However, if the results of the included studies in the meta-analysis are a biased sample of the studies, then the bias will also be transmitted to the meta-analysis results. Its obvious that studies that report a larger effect size or positive findings are more likely to be published than those reported smaller effect size or negative findings. This phenomenon is generally known as publication bias and refers to the selective publication of research studies based on their results.

Publication bias occurs when the publication of research results depends not just on the quality of the research but also on the hypothesis tested, and the significance and direction of the effects. The subject was first introduced in 1959 by statistician Theodore Sterling to discuss that "successful" research (providing positive result) is more likely to be published.

Why publication bias happens?

Publication bias is due to the fact that the number of included studies in the meta-analysis is not the same as the number that has to be included [1].

Many factors may contribute to publication bias. Sometimes researchers do not systematically search all databases and they miss some of the potential studies. On the other hand, studies with small sample sizes or negative results would not be published [2].

Researchers often do not submit their negative findings to the journals because they think that their research has failed to show a relationship or effects or the results are not interesting enough. Researchers may suppress negative clinical trial results for fear of losing their funding. Researchers know that if they submit positive results, their research is more likely to be published in a reputable journal. This increases your reputation among your colleagues, increases the number of citations of your paper, and increases your chances of getting more grants. On the other hand, studies

Systematic Review and Meta-Analysis. https://doi.org/10.1016/B978-0-443-13428-9.00012-4

with negative findings are cited less than studies with positive findings, so it is more attractive for journals to publish positive findings.

Importance of publication bias

Publication bias has been identified as a crucial threat in medical research for several years. Assessing the publication bias is an important topic in meta-analyses. Published studies are no longer a representative sample of the available evidence where publication bias is present. This bias distorts the results of systematic reviews and meta-analyses. Systematic reviews and meta-analyses can account for publication bias by including evidence from unpublished studies and the gray literature. It should also be noted that the results from published studies differ systematically from results of unpublished studies. Publication bias will result in misleading estimates of treatment effects. Publication bias in all basic biomedical research studies, observational, and clinical trials leads to invalid results. Overestimating the efficacy of a therapeutic intervention due to publication bias means will lead to excess cost without corresponding improvement in outcome.

Assessment of publication bias in meta-analyses

The presence of publication bias can also be explored by drawing a funnel plot in which the estimate of the reported effect size is plotted against the inverse of the square of the standard error (a measure of the precision of the studies). The premise is that the scatter of points should reflect a funnel shape, indicating that the reporting of effect sizes is not related to their statistical significance. However, when small studies are predominately in one direction (usually the direction of larger effect sizes), asymmetry will ensue and this may be indicative of publication bias. Because an inevitable degree of subjectivity exists in the interpretation of funnel plots, statistical tests have been proposed to detect funnel plot asymmetry. These tests are often based on linear regression including the Egger's regression asymmetry test (alongside the Begg's adjusted rank correlation test), and may adopt a multiplicative or additive dispersion parameter to adjust for the presence of between-study heterogeneity. Some approaches may even attempt to compensate for the (potential) presence of publication bias, which is particularly useful to explore the potential impact on meta-analysis results. Note that it is challenging to assess publication bias when the number of studies included in the meta-analysis is less than 10, and therefore it is not necessary to assess it.

Funnel plot

A funnel plot is a graphical illustration of eligible studies for inclusion in a meta-analysis and is used to detect suspected publication bias using visual analysis.

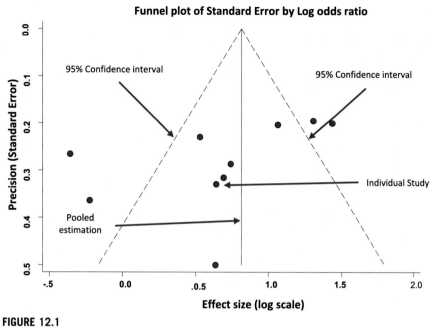

FIGURE 12.1

Funnel plot.

Here, a funnel plot is a simple scatterplot showing the relation between individual study's effect size (e.g., mean difference, odds ratio, or risk ratio) and its precision or some measure of each study's sample size. Most often, the horizontal axis (X) represents the individual effect-size estimates that range from small effect sizes located on the left side of the X axis to large effect sizes located on the right side of the X axis. The Y axis represents the individual study precision or standard error (SE) that ranges from a large standard error at the bottom of the Y axis to a small standard error at the top of the Y axis (Fig. 12.1). If the measure of effect is a ratio measure (such as OR, RR), the x-axis is displayed on log scale. In the absence of missing studies, the shape of the scatter plot should resemble a symmetrical inverted funnel with a wide base (consisting of small studies with large effect size variability) and a narrow top (consisting of large studies with small effect size variability). When publication bias occurs, we would expect an asymmetry in the distribution of small studies, with more studies showing positive results than negative results. The hypothetical funnel plot is shown in Fig. 12.1.

Begg's adjusted rank correlation test

A statistical test was proposed to test the presence of publication bias and avoid subjective interpretation of funnel plots. This test calculates and reports Kendall's nonparametric correlation coefficient between the standardized effect size and the corresponding standard error in different studies. In other words, this test interprets the funnel plot using a statistical method. This coefficient is interpreted the same as other correlation coefficients. If the funnel diagram is symmetrical and there is no publication bias in the results, this coefficient will be zero or close to zero, and its corresponding *P*-value will not be significant. Since the rank correlation tests are known to have low power, the significance level for this test should be ≤ 0.10. A positive correlation coefficient means a positive relationship between the effect sizes and standard errors (Fig. 12.2). The funnel plot for Begg's test is displayed horizontally as follows. When the funnel plot is asymmetric, and the correlation coefficient is positive, we expect small studies to have large standard errors and large effect sizes. On the contrary, when the coefficient is negative, it indicates that large studies with small standard errors have large standardized effect sizes.

One of the most common methods to assess publication bias is the Egger test, which is determined by regressing the standardized effect size on the inverse

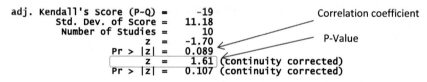

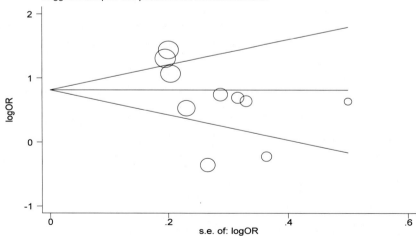

FIGURE 12.2

Begg's adjusted rank correlation test.

Egger's test

Std_Eff	Coef.	Std. Err.	t	P>|t|	[95% Conf. Interval]	
slope	2.010645	.6261925	3.21	0.012	.5666429	3.454648
bias	-4.810242	2.435738	-1.97	0.084	-10.42706	.8065789

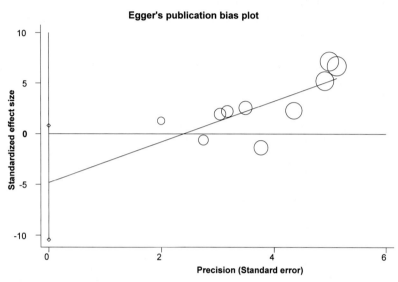

Egger's publication bias plot

FIGURE 12.3

Egger's regression asymmetry test.

standard error (precision). When there is no asymmetry in the plot, the regression line is expected to go through the origin (intercept or $\alpha = 0$). Intercept or $\alpha = 0$ is a test for the asymmetry of funnel plot, and the size of α indicates the extent of asymmetry. In meta-analyses, the P-value of Egger's regression test is usually reported. It should be noted that the statistical power of Egger's test is higher than Begg's test and it shows the possibility of publication bias better than Egger's test. Therefore, when the number of included studies in the meta-analysis is low, the use of the Egger's test is recommended (Fig. 12.3).

Trim and fill method

When potential publication bias is identified in a meta-analysis, it is desirable to adjust it. Trim and fill method was proposed by Duval and Tweedie in 2000 and is a complementary analysis to the funnel plot. It was developed to deal with asymmetry in the funnel plot. Briefly, in this two-step method derived from the funnel plot, the studies that caused the asymmetry of the funnel plot are estimated and "trimmed", then the true center of the funnel is estimated based on the remaining studies (symmetric parts). Next, the trimmed studies are added back, but are "filled" to the other side of the center. In other words, the funnel plot is repeated and the excluded studies are replaced with their "missing" counterparts around the adjusted summary estimate. Software's such as Stata, which has the ability to asses for publication bias through trim and fill methods, can create a funnel plot that includes both observed and imputed studies.

For our example in Chapter 10 regarding the odds of developing MS in cases with vitamin d deficiency, we need to apply logarithmic values of ORs and SEs of lnOR.

To obtain funnel plot, we have to type this command in stata:

metafunnel lnor seor.

To obtain lnor, we have to type this command:

gen lnor = ln(OR),

and for se(lnor) we have to obtain logarithmic values of upper and lower limits of confidence interval of OR:

So we have to type:

gen ulor = ln(UL),gen llor = ln(LL).

Selnor=(ulor-llor)/4.

In the hypothetical example (Fig. 12.4), the odds ratio (in log scale) as the desired effect size is located on the X axis, and the precision or standard error is on the Y

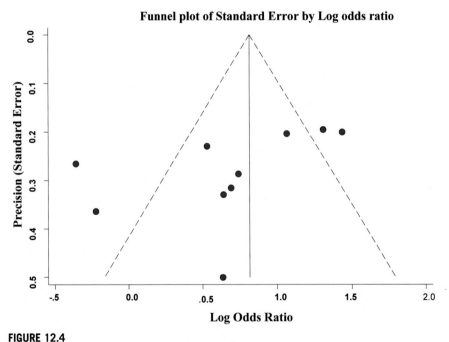

FIGURE 12.4

Funnel plot for OR of developing MS and vitamin d deficiency.

axis. Slight asymmetric distribution of effect sizes indicates the possibility of publication bias in is low. The result of the Begg's adjusted rank correlation test (Fig. 12.5) and Egger's regression asymmetry test (Fig. 12.6); indicate negligible possibility of publication bias.

To obtain Begg's test results, we have to type this command:
metabias LnOR seor,beg.
and for Egger's test, we have to type:
metabias LnOR seor, egger.
To obtain trim and fill results, we have to type: metatrim LnOR seor.

Begg's Test

Adj. Kendall's Score (P-Q) =   -19
Std. Dev. of Score = 11.18
Number of Studies =   10
z = **-1.70**
Pr > |z| = 0.089
z =   1.61 (continuity corrected)
Pr > |z| = 0.107 (continuity corrected)

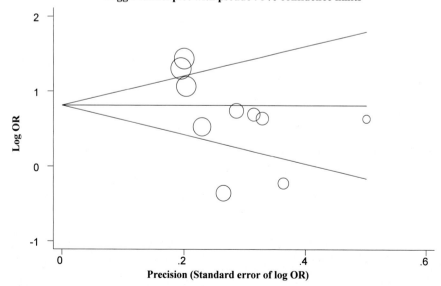

Begg's funnel plot with pseudo 95% confidence limits

FIGURE 12.5

Beggs's test and Begg's' funnel plot.

Egger's test

Std_Eff	Coef.	Std. Err.	t	P>|t|	[95% Conf. Interval]
Slope	2.010645	0.6261925	3.21	0.012	.5666429 3.454648
Bias	**-4.810242**	2.435738	-1.97	**0.084**	-10.42706 .8065789

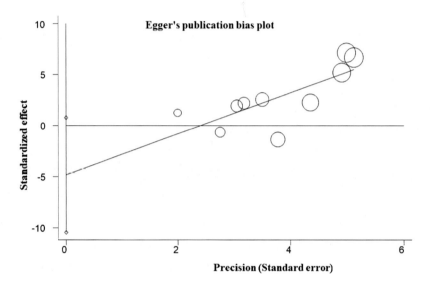

FIGURE 12.6

Egger's test and Egger's' plot.

The Duval and Tweedie's Trim and Fill method was used in order to quantify the magnitude of the publication bias, and also adjust the final results of the meta-analysis. Adjustment for publication bias with trim and fill method is not able to detect hypothetical negative unpublished studies, which influences the pooled estimation of the meta-analysis (Fig. 12.7). In our example, no missing study was identified and based on adjusted estimation, pooled odds ratio using random effects meta-analysis (0.67) before and after trimming is the same.

Funnel plot for standardized mean difference (SMD)

To obtain funnel plot for SMD, we have to obtain SMD and its se first.

The command will be:

metan n_1 mean$_1$ sd$_1$ n_2 mean$_2$ sd$_2$

Meta-analysis

Method	Pooled Est	95% CI Lower	Upper	Asymptotic z_value	p_value	No. of studies
Fixed	0.816	0.657	0.975	10.038	0.000	**10**
Random	**0.678**	**0.300**	**1.056**	3.515	0.000	

Test for heterogeneity: Q= 47.191 on 9 degrees of freedom (p= 0.000)
Moment-based estimate of between studies variance = 0.288

Trimming estimator: Linear
Meta-analysis type: Random-effects model

iteration	estimate	Tn	# to trim	diff
1	0.678	26	0	55
2	0.678	26	0	0

Filled

Meta-analysis

Method	Pooled Est	95% CI Lower	Upper	Asymptotic z_value	p_value	No. of studies
Fixed	0.816	0.657	0.975	10.038	0.000	10
Random	**0.678**	**0.300**	**1.056**	3.515	0.000	

Test for heterogeneity: Q= 47.191 on 9 degrees of freedom (p= 0.000)
Moment-based estimate of between studies variance = 0.288

FIGURE 12.7

The trim and fill method in the hypothetical example.

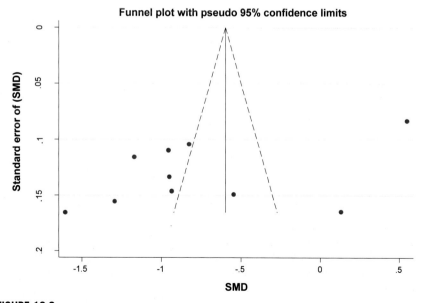

FIGURE 12.8

Funnelplot for SMD.

```
. metabias _ES _seES,begg

Note: data input format theta se_theta assumed.

Begg's test for small-study effects:
Rank correlation between standardized intervention effect and its standard error

    adj. Kendall's Score (P-Q) =      -9
             Std. Dev. of Score =   11.18
             Number of Studies =      10
                             z =   -0.80
                      Pr > |z| =    0.421
                             z =    0.72 (continuity corrected)
                      Pr > |z| =    0.474 (continuity corrected)
```

FIGURE 12.9

Begg test results.

Now, we will have new variables in stata regarding SMD and its se.
Then we can type:
metafunnel ES seES.
Regarding the mean difference as effect size (Fig. 12.8), slight asymmetry is observed in the visual inspection of the funnel plot and we can even say that the results of studies with small sample size have been published more often. However as shown in Figs. 12.9 and 12.10, Begg's and Egger's regression asymmetry tests are not statistically significant), which indicate no possibility of publication bias.

```
. metabias _ES _seES,egger

Note: data input format theta se_theta assumed.

Egger's test for small-study effects:
Regress standard normal deviate of intervention
effect estimate against its standard error

Number of studies =  10                      Root MSE     =   5.145
```

Std_Eff	Coef.	Std. Err.	t	P>|t|	[95% Conf. Interval]	
slope	1.141093	.8875132	1.29	0.235	-.9055158	3.187702
bias	-14.45812	7.190532	-2.01	0.079	-31.03952	2.123275

```
Test of H0: no small-study effects        P = 0.079
```

FIGURE 12.10

Egger's test results.

Trim and fill method did not identify any missing studies (Fig. 12.11). Pooled SMD of primary meta-analysis and trim and fill method were the same (−0.597), which indicates that publication bias is unlikely.

In general, publication bias is unfortunately unavoidable in systematic review and meta-analyses. Assessment of publication bias should become more routine as we move forward, although the suggested statistical tests are not able to identify this bias due to their low power.

```
. metatrim _ES _seES

Note: default data input format (theta, se_theta) assumed.

Meta-analysis

         |  Pooled      95% CI        Asymptotic       No. of
Method |     Est   Lower   Upper   z_value  p_value    studies
-------+----------------------------------------------------
Fixed  |  -0.597  -0.674  -0.521  -15.300   0.000       10
Random |  -0.758  -1.221  -0.295   -3.211   0.001

Test for heterogeneity: Q= 318.798 on 9 degrees of freedom (p= 0.000)
Moment-based estimate of between studies variance =  0.539


Trimming estimator: Linear
Meta-analysis type: Fixed-effects model

iteration |  estimate    Tn   # to trim    diff
----------+-----------------------------------------
     1    |   -0.597     19       0         55
     2    |   -0.597     19       0          0


Note: no trimming performed; data unchanged


Filled
Meta-analysis

         |  Pooled      95% CI        Asymptotic       No. of
Method |     Est   Lower   Upper   z_value  p_value    studies
-------+----------------------------------------------------
Fixed  |  -0.597  -0.674  -0.521  -15.300   0.000       10
Random |  -0.758  -1.221  -0.295   -3.211   0.001

Test for heterogeneity: Q= 318.798 on 9 degrees of freedom (p= 0.000)
Moment-based estimate of between studies variance =  0.539
```

FIGURE 12.11

Trim and fill results.

References

[1] Simmonds M. Quantifying the risk of error when interpreting funnel plots. Syst Rev 2015;4:1−7.

[2] Shi L, Lin L. The trim-and-fill method for publication bias: practical guidelines and recommendations based on a large database of meta-analyses. Medicine 2019;98(23): e15987.

Further reading

[1] Duval S, Tweedie R. A nonparametric "trim and fill" method of accounting for publication bias in meta-analysis. J Am Stat Assoc 2000a;95:89−98.

[2] Duval S, Tweedie R. Trim and fill: a simple funnel-plot−based method of testing and adjusting for publication bias in meta-analysis. Biometrics 2000b;56:455−63.

[3] Egger M, Davey Smith G, Schneider M, Minder C. Bias in meta-analysis detected by a simple, graphical test. BMJ 1997;315:629−34.

[4] Begg CB, Mazumdar M. Operating characteristics of a rank correlation test for publication bias. Biometrics 1994;50:1088−101.

[5] Lin L, Chu H. Quantifying publication bias in meta-analysis. Biometrics 2018;74(3): 785−94.

[6] Mavridis D, Salanti G. How to assess publication bias: funnel plot, trim-and-fill method and selection models. BMJ Ment Health 2014;17(1):30.

[7] Song F, Hooper L, Loke YK. Publication bias: what is it? How do we measure it? How do we avoid it? Open Access J Clin Trials 2013:71−81.

[8] McShane BB, Böckenholt U, Hansen KT. Adjusting for publication bias in meta-analysis: an evaluation of selection methods and some cautionary notes. Perspect Psychol Sci 2016;11(5):730−49.

[9] Mavridis D, Salanti G. Exploring and accounting for publication bias in mental health: a brief overview of methods. BMJ Ment Health 2014;17(1):11−5.

[10] Fisher DJ, Zwahlen M, Egger M, Higgins JP. Meta-analysis in stata. In: Systematic reviews in health research: meta-analysis in context; 2022. p. 481−509.

[11] Chaimani A, Mavridis D, Salanti G. A hands-on practical tutorial on performing meta-analysis with Stata. BMJ Ment Health 2014;17(4):111−6.

[12] Cumpston M, Li T, Page MJ, Chandler J, Welch VA, Higgins JP, Thomas J. Updated guidance for trusted systematic reviews: a new edition of the Cochrane Handbook for Systematic Reviews of Interventions. Cochrane Database Syst Rev 2019;2019(10).

[13] Rothstein HR, Sutton AJ, Borenstein M. Publication bias in meta-analysis. In: Publication bias in meta-analysis: prevention, assessment and adjustments; 2005. p. 1−7.

[14] Borenstein M, Hedges LV, Higgins JP, Rothstein HR. Introduction to meta-analysis. John Wiley & Sons; 2021.

[15] Jin ZC, Zhou XH, He J. Statistical methods for dealing with publication bias in meta-analysis. Stat Med 2015;34(2):343−60.

[16] Song E, Gilbody D. Publication and related biases. Health Technol Assess 2000;4(10).

[17] Afonso J, Ramirez-Campillo R, Clemente FM, Büttner FC, Andrade R. The perils of misinterpreting and misusing "publication bias" in meta-analyses: an education review on funnel plot-based methods. Sports Med September 2023;8:1−3.

Heterogeneity among included studies

Mehdi Mokhtari

Department of Epidemiology, Khoy University of Medical Science, Khoy, Iran

Why measure heterogeneity in meta-analysis?

Measuring heterogeneity in meta-analysis is essential to determine whether the studies are sufficiently similar or comparable with be pooled together. Measuring heterogeneity also helps to identify the sources and causes of heterogeneity and to explore the potential moderators or subgroups that can be the source of the heterogeneity between study results.

How to measure heterogeneity in meta-analysis?

There are two main approaches to measure heterogeneity in meta-analysis: visual inspection and statistical tests. Visual inspection involves examining the graphical displays of the study results, such as forest plots. Visual inspection can help to detect outliers, asymmetry, or patterns of heterogeneity. However, visual inspection is subjective and may not capture the magnitude or significance of heterogeneity. Statistical tests involve calculating numerical indices or values that quantify the degree or probability of heterogeneity. Statistical tests can help to assess the magnitude or significance of heterogeneity objectively and precisely.

Introduction

We know that the goal of a synthesis is not simply to compute a summary effect, but rather to make sense of the pattern of effects. An intervention that consistently reduces the risk of criminal behavior by 40% across a range of studies is very different from one that reduces the risk by 40% on average with a risk reduction that ranges from 10% in some studies to 70% in others. The extent of heterogeneity in a meta-analysis partly determines the difficulty in drawing overall conclusions. This extent may be measured by estimating a between-study variance, but interpretation is then specific to a particular treatment effect metric [1].

Addressing statistical heterogeneity is one of the most troublesome aspects of many systematic reviews. The interpretative problems depend on how substantial

Systematic Review and Meta-Analysis. https://doi.org/10.1016/B978-0-443-13428-9.00013-6

the heterogeneity is, since this determines the extent to which it might influence the conclusions of the meta-analysis. It is therefore important to be able to quantify the extent of heterogeneity among a collection of studies. We have to estimate the between-study variance of the parameters of interest in included studies. The variance can be used to describe the extent of variability in the included effect size across studies.

What is heterogeneity?

In reality, studies that are included in a systematic review will differ. Any kind of variability among studies in a systematic review may be termed heterogeneity. It can be helpful to distinguish between different types of heterogeneity. Variability in the participants, interventions and outcomes of interest may be described as clinical diversity (sometimes called clinical heterogeneity), and variability in study design, outcome measurement tools and risk of bias may be described as methodological diversity (sometimes called methodological heterogeneity). Variability in the intervention effects being evaluated in the different studies is known as statistical heterogeneity, and is a consequence of clinical or methodological diversity, or both. We will follow convention and refer to statistical heterogeneity simply as heterogeneity.

Clinical variation will lead to heterogeneity if the intervention effect is affected by the factors that vary across studies. In other words, the true intervention effect will be different in different studies.

Differences between included studies in terms of methodological factors, such as blinding and concealment of allocation sequence, or differences between studies regarding the definition of outcomes and their measurements, may lead to different reported effects. Significant statistical heterogeneity is arising from methodological diversity or outcome assessments differences and suggesting that the studies are not estimating the same measure, but does not necessarily show that the true intervention effect varies. In particular, heterogeneity associated solely with methodological diversity would indicate that the studies suffer from different degrees of bias. Empirical evidence suggests that some aspects of design can affect the result of clinical trials, although this is not always the case.

Meta-analysis should only be considered when a group of studies is sufficiently homogeneous in terms of participants, interventions, and outcomes to provide a meaningful summary. A common analogy is that sometimes systematic reviews bring together apples and oranges, and that combining these can yield a meaningless result. This is true if apples and oranges are of intrinsic interest on their own, but may not be combined if they are used to contribute to a wider question regarding the fruits.

It is generally accepted that meta-analyses should assess heterogeneity, which may be defined as the presence of variation in true effect sizes underlying the different studies. This assessment might be achieved by performing a statistical test for heterogeneity, by quantifying its magnitude, by quantifying its impact or by a combination of these. Heterogeneity is to be expected in a meta-analysis: it would be surprising if multiple studies, performed by different teams in different places with different methods, all ended up estimating the same underlying parameter. From the standpoint that heterogeneity is inevitable in a meta-analysis, we are left with the question of whether there is an 'acceptable' degree of heterogeneity. The challenge is then to decide on the most appropriate way to analyses heterogeneous studies, and this will depend on the aims of the synthesis and, to an extent, the observed directions and magnitudes of effects.

Heterogeneity in a primary study

The basic idea of heterogeneity in a meta-analysis is similar to that in a primary study. Consider a primary study to assess the distribution of math scores in a high-school class. Suppose that the mean score across all students in the class is 50. To understand how the students are performing, we also need to ask about heterogeneity, and we typically do so by reporting the standard deviation of scores. We understand that 95% of all students will score within two standard deviations of the mean.

Therefore,

A. If the standard deviation is 5 points, most students will score between 40 and 60,
B. If the standard deviation is 10 points, most students will score between 30 and 70,
C. If the standard deviation is 20 points, most students will score between 10 and 90.

These intervals are called prediction intervals.

When we perform a primary study, we compute several other statistics related to heterogeneity, such as the sum of squares and the variance. These are all important statistics, but if we want to know how much the scores vary, these statistics are tangential, at best. The best statistics that directly address this question are the standard deviation and prediction interval [2].

Heterogeneity in a meta-analysis

The same ideas apply when we turn to meta-analysis. For example, consider the following [3]: conduct a meta-analysis of 17 studies to assess the impact of methylphenidate in adults with Attention Deficit Hyperactivity Disorder (ADHD). Patients with this disorder have trouble performing cognitive tasks, and it was hypothesized that the drug would improve their cognitive function. Patients were randomized to receive either the drug or a placebo, and then tested on measures of cognitive function. The effect size was the standardized mean difference between groups on the measure of cognitive function.

In this context,

- A standardized mean difference of 0.20 would represent a trivial effect size. While this difference would be captured by the test, it is so small that the patient might not be aware of any change.
- A standardized mean difference of 0.50 would represent a moderate effect size. The patient would be aware of a clinically important change, and some co-workers might notice the change as well.
- A standardized mean difference of 0.80 would represent a large effect size. The patient would be pleasantly surprised by the improvement, and some coworkers would be likely to remark that something was different.

It turns out that the mean effect size is 0.50. On average, across all comparable populations, the drug increases cognitive functioning by one-half a standard deviation. But to understand the potential utility of the drug we also need to ask about heterogeneity.

Identifying and quantifying heterogeneity

The mechanisms for describing the variation among scores in a primary study are well known. We can compute the standard deviation of the scores and discuss the proportion of subjects falling within a given range. We can compute the variance of the scores and discuss what proportion of variance can be explained by covariates.

Our goals are similar in a meta-analysis, in the sense that we want to describe the variation, using indices such as the standard deviation and variance. However, the process is more complicated for the following reason. However, the variation that we actually observe is partly spurious, incorporating both (true) heterogeneity and also random error.

To understand the problem, suppose that all studies in the analysis shared the same true effect size, so that the (true) heterogeneity is zero. Under this assumption, we would not expect the observed effects to be identical to each other.

Now, assume that the true effect size does vary from one study to the other. In this case, the observed effects vary from one another for two reasons. One is the real heterogeneity in effect size, and the other is the within-study errors.

To extract the true between-studies variation from the observed variation you can:

1. Compute the total amount of study-to-study variation actually observed.
2. Estimate how much the observed effects would be expected to vary from each other if the true effect was actually the same in all studies.
3. The excess variation (if any) is assumed to reflect real differences in effect size (that is, the heterogeneity).

Consider the top row in Fig. 13.1. The observed effects (and therefore variation in the observed effects) are identical in A and B. The difference between A and B is that the confidence intervals. For each study in A, the CIS are relatively wide, while the confidence intervals for each study in B are relatively narrow.

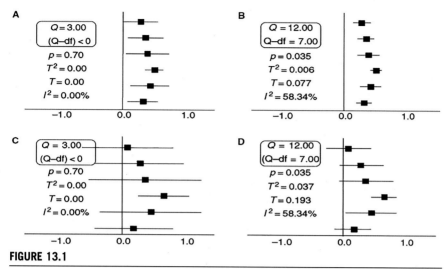

FIGURE 13.1

Cochran's Q.

In other words, we need a statistic that is sensitive to the ratio of the observed variation to the within-study error, rather than their absolute values.

The statistic that we use for this purpose is Q.

Cochran's Q

The most common statistical tests for heterogeneity in meta-analysis are the Q test, the I2 statistic, and the tau-squared statistic. The Q test compares the observed variation among the study results with the expected variation due to sampling error. The Q test produces a *P*-value that indicates the probability of observing such variation by chance. A low *P*-value (usually less than 0.05 or 0.1) suggests significant heterogeneity. However, the Q test has low power to detect heterogeneity when the number of studies is small or the effect sizes are large.

The formula is:

$$Q = \sum_{i=1}^{k} W_i(Y_i - M)^2$$

Where Wi is the study weight (1/Vi), Yi is the study effect size, M is the summary effect, and k is the number of studies. We compute the deviation of each effect size from the mean, square it, then we weigh it by the inverse-variance method, and finally sum all of these values to yield the weighted sum of squares (WSS), or Q.

The equal formula is:

$$Q = \sum_{i=1}^{k} \left(\frac{Y_i - M}{S_i}\right)^2$$

Finally, the other formula, which is useful for computations, is:

$$Q = \sum_{i=1}^{k} W_i Y_i^2 - \left(\frac{\left(\sum_{i=1}^{k} W_i Y_i \right)^2}{\sum_{i=1}^{k} W_i} \right)$$

The next step is to determine the expected value of Q on the assumption that all studies share a common effect size, and if there is any variation, it is due to sampling error. The degrees of freedom (df),

$$df = k - 1,$$

where k is the number of studies.

The excess variation

Since Q is the observed WSS, and df is the expected WSS (under the assumption that all studies share a common effect), the difference:

$$Q-df,$$

Reflects the excess variation, the part that will be attributed to differences in the true effects from study to study.

Ratio of observed to expected variation

Earlier, we used Fig. 13.1 to introduce the concept of excess variation, and showed that it is based on the ratio of observed variance to the within study variance. In Fig. 13.1 we have the same four plots plus Cochran's Q, which quantifies this concept.

First, consider the top row. For plot A the observed value of Q is 3.00, versus an expected value (under the assumption of a common effect size) of 5.00 (that is, k_1). In this case the observed variation is less than the expected value. For plot B the observed value of Q is 12.00, versus an expected value of 5.00, so the observed variation is greater than we would expect based on within-study error (Q is greater than the degrees of freedom). This finding is consistent with the visual impression. For plot C the observed value of Q is 3.00, versus an expected value of 5.00, (Q < df) and for plot D the observed value of Q is 12.00, versus an expected value of 5.00, (Q > df). Note that Q is the same (3.00) in A and C because these plots share the same ratio, except that the absolute range of effects is higher in C. Similarly, the value of Q is the same (12.00) in B and D because these plots share the same ratio, despite the fact that the absolute range of effects is higher in D.

Detecting heterogeneity

Several strategies have been used to assess heterogeneity. The simplest option is an inspection of the forest plot to see if the point estimates differ between studies and if

CIs have high or less overlaps [4]. Sometimes differences may be hard to detect by visual inspection. One of the measures that quantifies Q is not interpreted as a measure of heterogeneity by itself. It is used to test the hypothesis that there is no heterogeneity, and *P*-values are reported. While this may be done, it should be noted that large *P*-values should not be interpreted as the absence of heterogeneity [4]. This test has low power, especially when there are few studies, a common situation in most meta-analyses.

I^2

The I^2 statistic estimates the proportion of the total variation among the study results that is due to heterogeneity rather than sampling error. The I^2 statistic ranges from 0% to 100%, with higher values indicating higher heterogeneity. There is no fixed threshold for interpreting the I^2 statistic, but some common guidelines are: 0%−25%: low heterogeneity; 25%−50%: moderate heterogeneity; 50%−75%: high heterogeneity; and 75%−100%: very high heterogeneity.

I^2 describes the magnitude of heterogeneity as the proportion of the total variability that is attributable to between-study variability. Cut-offs have been proposed but noted to be not applicable in all circumstances [2,4]. However, there is an agreement in the importance of reporting confidence intervals of I^2 for proper interpretation [2,5]. Whatever numerical measure of heterogeneity is used, this should be interpreted together with a visual inspection. Numerical measures should not replace visual inspection but should complement it.

$$I^2 = \frac{Q - df}{Q}$$

Q is total sum of squares, df is the sum of squares that is attributable to sampling error. In the denominator, we have Q again, so I^2 is the ratio of true to total heterogeneity.

Tau square (Tau²)

The tau-squared statistic estimates the variance of the true effect sizes across the studies. The tau-squared statistic reflects the absolute amount of heterogeneity, and can be used to calculate the confidence intervals and prediction intervals of the meta-analysis results.

Methodological options to explore heterogeneity

As mentioned before, random-effects models should be preferred in the presence of significant heterogeneity [6]. Still, other options can be used to minimize the effects of heterogeneity on the meta-analytic value. The most commonly used methodological options are sensitivity analysis, subgroup meta-analysis, and meta-regression [7−9].

Sensitivity analyses seek to explore the impact of different decisions on the outcomes/meta-analysis. These types of analyses may explore the impact of using different meta-analysis models or of excluding or including studies in meta-analyses based on sample size, methodological quality, or variance. If results remain consistent across different analyses, they can be considered robust. In opposition, different results across sensitivity analyses indicate that the results should be interpreted with caution and/or targeted for corrective action [8,9].

On the other hand, subgroup meta-analysis allows drawing valid conclusions from meta-analyses of heterogeneous studies when they are subgrouped (i.e., the results of the individual studies within each subgroup are similar) [10]. In addition, the analyses, in some cases, require presentation by groups due to the clinical sense. For example, it may be necessary to estimate the effectiveness of the treatment for specific subgroups of patients (characteristics: gender, age, among others) or even of the intervention (type, dose, frequency, intensity, route of administration, among others) [7,10].

There may be five scenarios in subgroup meta-analyses: (1) There is a statistically significant, quantitative subgroup effect; (2) there is a statistically significant, qualitative subgroup effect, with substantial unexplained heterogeneity; (3) there is no subgroup effect; (4) there is no subgroup effect, but there is unexplained heterogeneity; and (5) there is a statistically significant subgroup effect, with an uneven covariate distribution [10]. Finally, if studies are divided into subgroups, meta-regression can help to explore the sources of heterogeneity. Meta-regression is an extension of subgroup analyses that allows investigating the effect of continuous or categorical characteristics and the effects of multiple factors. Meta-regressions are similar in essence to simple regressions, in which an outcome/dependent variable is predicted according to the values of one or more explanatory variables. In meta-regression, the outcome variable is the effect estimate (for example, a mean difference, a risk difference). Explanatory variables are characteristics of studies that can influence the size of the intervention effect and are often referred to as 'potential effect modifiers' or covariates [9].

Subgroup analysis

When heterogeneity is found in a meta-analysis it is important to examine potential sources of this heterogeneity. One of the most used methods to examine sources of heterogeneity is the so-called 'subgroup analysis' [11,12]. In a subgroup analysis, the included studies are divided into two or more subgroups, and it is tested whether the pooled effect sizes found in these subgroups differ significantly from each other by looking at the interaction between the subgroup and the treatment [13]. Subgroup analyses can be considered as a core component of most published meta-analyses and are recommended by the Cochrane Handbook for meta-analyses [14].

Subgroup analyses are, however, associated with several important methodological problems [11,12]. One important problem of subgroup analyses is that they are easily interpreted causally, while the results are in fact observational [14]. Participants in the interventions are not randomized to one of the subgroups, which means that these results cannot be interpreted in a causal way. If for example an intervention is found to be more effective in nursing homes than in other settings, this can indicate a real difference between settings, but not that nursing homes reduce the effect size estimates. For example, it can also be related to the age of participants or that in nursing homes more single persons live than in other settings. Especially when the number of studies is limited, the characteristics of the included studies can be highly correlated with each other and it would be difficult to reason what the actual causes of the subgroup differences are.

Meta-regression to explain heterogeneity

Ideally, possible sources of clinical or methodological heterogeneity should be identified before the results are pooled in a meta-analysis, based on a review of the included studies' demographics and methodology, as well as application to known pharmacological and (patho) physiological phenomenon [15]. There should generally be a sound rationale when deciding to undertake a meta-regression, not simply because the results of a meta-analysis were suggestive that an association might exist or because the ability to run multiple unfounded meta-regressions exists [15,16]. In the B&S [17] example, it would be difficult to justify a meta-regression examining the effect of year of publication on the incidence of cancer with pravastatin use, as it is unlikely that pravastatin's propensity to cause cancer changed from year-to-year. Consequently, even covariates defined a priori need to be considered hypothesis generating rather than being definitive.

Dealing with heterogeneity

When heterogeneity is low, the pooled estimate can consider only within-study variation (fixed-effect model). If heterogeneity is detected, an explanation should be sought. The populations may vary (based on ages and nutritional status in the zinc example), the interventions may not be exactly the same (zinc varies in dose and formulation), the outcome measures may be different (different standardization of preweighted disposable diapers to measure stool output), or the study designs may be dissimilar (randomized by individuals or by clusters) [4,18]. Subgroup analysis or meta-regression using study-level characteristics could be done.

Choosing between fixed and random effects models

If there is very little variation between trials, then I^2 will be low and a fixed effects model might be appropriate. With fixed effects, the only difference between studies is their power to detect the outcome of interest. An alternative approach, 'random effects', allows the study outcomes to vary between studies. Many investigators consider the random effects approach to be a more natural choice than fixed effects [19–21].

More data are required for random effects models to achieve the same statistical power as fixed effects models, and there is no 'exact' way to handle studies with small numbers using random effects. This should not be a problem with most meta-analyses.

References

[1] Higgins JP, Thompson SG. Quantifying heterogeneity in a meta-analysis. Stat Med June 15, 2002;21(11):1539–58. https://doi.org/10.1002/sim.1186.

[2] Higgins JPT, Thompson SG, Deeks JJ, Altman DG. Measuring inconsistency in meta-analyses. BMJ 2003;327(7414):557–60. https://doi.org/10.1136/bmj.327.7414.557. PMID: 12958120; PMCID: PMC192859.

[3] Castells X, Ramos-Quiroga JA, Rigau D, Bosch R, Nogueira M, Vidal X, Casas M. Efficacy of methylphenidate for adults with attention-deficit hyperactivity disorder: a meta-regression analysis. CNS Drugs 2011;25(2):157–69.

[4] Deeks JJ, Higgins JPT, Altman DG, Green S, editors. Cochrane handbook for systematic reviews of interventions. Version 5.1.0. Chichester, West Sussex; Hoboken NJ: John Wiley & Sons; 2008.

[5] Loannidis J, Patsopoulos N, Evangelou E. Uncertainty in heterogeneity estimate in meta-analyses. BMJ 2007;335:914e6.

[6] Tufanaru C, Munn Z, Stephenson M, Aromataris E. Fixed or random effects meta-analysis? Common methodological issues in systematic reviews of effectiveness. Internl J Evidence-Based Health 2015;13(3):196–207. https://doi.org/10.1097/xeb.0000000000000065.

[7] Santos EJ, Cunha M. Interpretação crítica dos resultados estatísticos de uma meta-análise: Estratégias metodológicas. Millenium 2013;44:85–98.

[8] Tufanaru C, Munn Z, Aromataris E, Campbell J, Hopp L. Systematic reviews of effectiveness. In: Aromataris E, Munn Z, editors. Joanna briggs institute reviewer's manual (chapter 3). The Joanna Briggs Institute; 2017.

[9] Higgins JPT, López-López JA, Becker BJ, Davies SR, Dawson S, Grimshaw JM, McGuinness LA, Moore THM, Rehfuess EA, Thomas J, Caldwell DM. Synthesising quantitative evidence in systematic reviews of complex health interventions. BMJ Glob Health 2019 Jan 25;4(Suppl 1):e000858. https://doi.org/10.1136/bmjgh-2018-000858. PMID: 30775014; PMCID: PMC6350707.

[10] Richardson M, Garner P, Donegan S. Interpretation of subgroup analyses in systematic reviews: a tutorial. Clin Epidemiol Global Health 2019;7(2):192–8. https://doi.org/10.1016/j.cegh.2018.05.005.

[11] Sun X, Briel M, Busse JW, You JJ, Akl EA, Mejza F, Bala MM, Bassler D, Mertz D, Diaz-Granados N, Vandvik PO, Malaga G, Srinathan SK, Dahm P, Johnston BC, Alonso-Coello P, Hassouneh B, Walter SD, Heels-Ansdell D, Bhatnagar N, Altman DG, Guyatt GH. Credibility of claims of subgroup effects in randomised controlled trials: systematic review. Br Med J 2012;344:e1553.

[12] Sun X, Ioannidis JP, Agoritsas T, Agoritsas T, Alba AC, Guyatt G. How to use a subgroup analysis: users' guide to the medical literature. J Am Med Assoc 2014;311:405–11.

[13] Cuijpers P. Meta-analyses in mental health research; A practical guide. Amsterdam: Vrije Universiteit; 2016. Available at: http://bit.do/meta-analysis [Google Scholar].

[14] Higgins JPT, Thomas J, Chandler J, Cumpston M, Li T, Page MJ, Welch VA, editors. Cochrane handbook for systematic reviews of interventions version 6.2 (updated february 2021). Cochrane; 2021. Available at: www.training.cochrane.org/handbook.

[15] Thompson SG, Sharp SJ. Explaining heterogeneity in meta-analysis: a comparison of methods. Stat Med 1999;18:2693–708.

[16] Wang R, Lagakos SW, Ware JH, Hunter DJ, Drazen JM. Statistics in medicine — reporting of subgroup analyses in clinical trials. N Engl J Med 2007;357:2189—94.

[17] Bonovas S, Sitaras NM. Does pravastatin promote cancer in elderly patients? A meta-analysis. CMAJ (Can Med Assoc J) 2007;176:649—54.

[18] Lazzerini M, Wanzira H. Oral zinc for treating diarrhea in children. Cochrane Database Syst Rev 2016;12:CD005436.

[19] Fleiss JL, Gross AJ. Meta-analysis in epidemiology, with special reference to studies of the association between exposure to environmental tobacco smoke and lung cancer: a critique. J Clin Epidemiol 1991;44:127—39.

[20] DerSimonian R, Laird N. Meta-analysis in clinical trials. Contr Clin Trials 1986;7:177—88.

[21] Ades AE, Higgins JPT. The interpretation of random-effects meta-analysis in decision models. Med Decis Making 2005;25:646—54.

Missing data in systematic reviews

14

Mohsen Rastkar

Tehran University of Medical Sciences, Tehran, Iran

Dealing with missing data is a common challenge in conducting systematic reviews and meta-analyses, which can affect the final results, and validity of the evidence. In a study, missing data might originate in the following means [1]:

1. Missing due to incomplete reporting of outcome: In some cases, there is no access to part of the study results because they are not reported by the researchers. For example, in a study, the results that show the side effects of a new medication may be less reported. As a result, it may alter the results of meta-analysis. This challenge of missing data is also related to publication bias, which shows that the researchers tend to publish only significant results of their studies. In this situation, the primary data of the study could be requested from the researchers of the study.

2. Missing due to reporting results in primary studies: in analyzing the aggregated data of included studies, one of the basic challenges is the type of data reported in the articles. In some primary studies, authors do not report necessary statistics, which we need in systematic reviews. For example, if authors only reported mean or median, and they didn't report standard deviation, interquartile range, or confidence intervals, the results cannot be used in the meta-analysis. This challenge could be resolved by extracting data from other parts of the article such as figures or asking the authors to send you the missing statistics.

3. Missing participants: In interventional or cohort studies, participants who are followed up may drop out of the study for various reasons before the final analysis. People who drop out of the study may be the same as the study group, or they may differ. For example, in a study, people who have less adherence to treatment and show less health-oriented behavior are missed. In this situation, according to the study, several hypotheses can be considered:

Missing completely at random: In this case, the people who are missing from the study are completely random.

Missing at random: By considering one or a few variables in the participants, the distribution of missing cases is random.

Missing not at random: If the missing people are not random, for example, they have worse consequences than the participants.

Systematic Review and Meta-Analysis. https://doi.org/10.1016/B978-0-443-13428-9.00014-8

When data that you needed for your analysis are missed, you can contact the corresponding authors of the original papers and ask them to send you the data that you need such as standard deviation, odds ratio, or raw data.

Reference

[1] Deeks JJ, Higgins JPT, Altman DG. Analysing data and undertaking meta-analyses. In: Cochrane handbook for systematic reviews of interventions. United Kingdom: wiley; 2019. p. 241—84. https://doi.org/10.1002/9781119536604.ch10.

Network meta-analysis

15

Mahsa Ghajarzadeh

Department of Neurology, Johns Hopkins University School of Medicine, Baltimore, MD, United States

What is network meta-analysis?

Systematic reviews of clinical trials are the best evidence for practice. When more than one study is available, systematic reviews could provide an overall estimate of the effect [1]. In reality, there are more than two treatments for most conditions, and direct pairwise comparisons of two treatments are not possible in all most all situations. When we have three treatments, we can have only three pairwise comparisons, while when we have five treatments, we could have 10 comparisons; with 10 interventions, the number of possible pairwise comparisons is 45 [2].

Network meta-analysis (NMA), which is called multiple treatment meta-analysis or mixed treatment comparisons, is developed recently and applies meta-analysis principles to assess multiple treatments in a single analysis by combining direct and indirect comparisons [3].

Suppose we have RTCs that compare treatment A with B and B with C. If we want to compare treatment A with C (indirect comparison), we can apply NMA (Fig. 15.1).

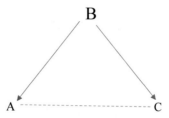

FIGURE 15.1

Indirect comparison of two treatments.

Steps of conducting NMA

The steps of conducting NMA are similar to the meta-analysis conduction.

Systematic Review and Meta-Analysis. https://doi.org/10.1016/B978-0-443-13428-9.00015-X

The first step is defining the review question and eligibility criteria

As for many systematic reviews, NMA question should be well defined before the initiation of the study.

The recommended approach for defining NMA question is participants, intervention, comparator, and outcome (PICO), which helps researchers frame their search strategy and process.

On the other hand, we have to determine the size of the network and the distinction of the treatments in the NMA before the study initiation [4].

Sensitive and comprehensive search

The search for NMA should be comprehensive and sensitive, which is broader than the search for systematic reviews (as the question is broader).

Data extraction and abstracting data of included studies

All included studies should be evaluated at least by two independent researchers, and data should be abstracted based on the study question.

Before analyzing data, we have to determine the geometry of the NMA, which shows which studies should be compared directly and which should be compared indirectly [5]. Network graph could be applied for network geometry (Fig. 15.2).

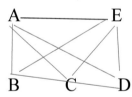

FIGURE 15.2

Network meta-analysis graph.

Qualitative evidence synthesis

Like systematic reviews, in all NMA, heterogeneity assessment (including clinical and methodological assessment) should be done, and transitivity (similarity on effect modifier in included studies) should be evaluated.

If age is an effect modifier, all potential studies should include patients with same age range.

Quantitative synthesis

Before conducting NMA, pairwise comparison of interventions should be done, and the statistical heterogeneity of each comparison should be calculated.

The next step is to determine the model of NMA which could be multivariate or hierarchical model [6]. The reference treatment which could be placebo or no treatment group or the most common treatment of the condition should be selected and all other treatments will be compared with the reference treatment. Summarized results as well as appropriate ranking statistics should be reported in this part.

NMA allows for comparison of the effect between different interventions, which will be presented as a square matrix (league table) [7]. NMA also provides results regarding ranking of the interventions. We can apply surface under the cumulative ranking curves (SUCRA) method to rank the interventions. The value of SUCRA presents the probability of being among the best treatment options [8].

Interpret results and draw conclusions

Interpret the results of NMA especially ranking statistics, and if you apply Grading of Recommendations, Assessment, Development, and Evaluations (GRADE) to evaluate the quality of NMA, please report the results in this section. The results of NMA should be interpreted carefully especially once interpreting the effectiveness and safety results, and if heterogeneity or inconsistency exists, poor-quality studies are included in NMA [3].

Report findings

The results of the systematic reviews as well as NMAs should be clear and transparent for patients, clinicians, and policy-makers. It is recommended to apply the Preferred Reporting Items for Systematic reviews and Meta-Analyses (PRISMA) statement to report the results transparent [9]. In this way, you provide all required details which could be applied by whom they needed them.

Conducting NMA is beyond the scope of this book.

References

[1] Dias S, Caldwell DM. Network meta-analysis explained. BMJ Publishing Group; 2019.
[2] Mayo-Wilson E, Dias S, Mavranezouli I, Kew K, Clark DM, Ades A, et al. Psychological and pharmacological interventions for social anxiety disorder in adults: a systematic review and network meta-analysis. Lancet Psychiatr 2014;1(5):368–76.
[3] Rouse B, Chaimani A, Li T. Network meta-analysis: an introduction for clinicians. Int Emerg Med 2017;12:103–11.
[4] Caldwell DM. An overview of conducting systematic reviews with network meta-analysis. Syst Rev 2014;3(1):109.
[5] Mills EJ, Thorlund K, Ioannidis JP. Demystifying trial networks and network meta-analysis. Br Med J 2013;346.
[6] White IR. Network meta-analysis. Stata J 2015;15(4):951–85.
[7] Mavridis D, Giannatsi M, Cipriani A, Salanti G. A primer on network meta-analysis with emphasis on mental health. BMJ Ment Health 2015;18(2):40–6.

[8] Salanti G, Ades A, Ioannidis JP. Graphical methods and numerical summaries for presenting results from multiple-treatment meta-analysis: an overview and tutorial. J Clin Epidemiol 2011;64(2):163–71.

[9] Moher D, Liberati A, Tetzlaff J, Altman DG, PRISMA Group* t. Preferred reporting items for systematic reviews and meta-analyses: the PRISMA statement. Ann Intern Med 2009;151(4):264–9.

Quality assessment of systematic reviews

16

Narges Ebrahimi[1,2]

[1]*Department of Immunology, Faculty of Medicine, Isfahan University of Medical Sciences, Isfahan, Iran;* [2]*Immunodeficiency Diseases Research Center, Isfahan University of Medical Sciences, Isfahan, Iran*

Rapid growth of medical literature as well as systematic reviews, increases the need for quality assessment of systematic reviews to see if you can rely on the results or not.

To evaluate the quality of systematic reviews, AMSTAR (Assessing the Methodological Quality of Systematic Reviews) tool was introduced in 2007 [1].

Q. 1: Did the research questions and inclusion criteria for the review include the components of PICO?

In the realm of systematic reviews, clarity and precision in defining research questions and inclusion criteria are fundamental. The first question in AMSTAR-2 serves as a litmus test for the systematic review's foundation, asking: **"Did the research questions and inclusion criteria for the review include the components of PICO?"**

PICO: a structured approach that dissects research queries into distinct components.

- **Population (P):** The specific group of individuals or patients the review aims to investigate,
- **Intervention (I):** The particular treatment, exposure, or intervention under study,
- **Comparison (C):** The alternative to the intervention, such as a placebo or different form of treatment, if applicable,
- **Outcome (O):** The anticipated results or effects of the intervention such as: quality of life.

We discussed about the PICO, its components, and its importance in Chapter 4.

Systematic Review and Meta-Analysis. https://doi.org/10.1016/B978-0-443-13428-9.00016-1

Q. 2: Did the report of the review contain an explicit statement that the review methods were established prior to the conduct of the review and did the report justify any significant deviations from the protocol?

Protocols: The blueprint for methodological rigor

Before embarking on a systematic review journey, researchers meticulously craft a protocol. This document serves as the foundational blueprint, outlining the review's design, objectives, inclusion criteria, data extraction methods, and analysis techniques. Establishing methods 'a priori' fosters transparency and guards against post hoc modifications, ensuring unbiased review process.

A hallmark of a high-quality systematic review is the methodology. This statement serves as an evidence to the review's methodological integrity, indicating that the research team adhered to a preestablished plan. However, significant deviations from the initial protocol might occur due to unforeseen circumstances, evolving methodologies, or the discovery of new information during the review process.

In such instances, it becomes imperative for the review report to provide clear and justified explanations for these deviations. Transparent reporting ensures that readers comprehend the rationale behind any alterations, preserving the review's credibility and allowing readers to evaluate the potential impact of these changes on the study's outcomes.

Why it matters: Upholding trust and reliability

For both creators and consumers of systematic reviews, understanding the adherence to established protocols and the rationale behind deviations is pivotal. Explicit statements and well-justified modifications bolster the review's trustworthiness. They signify a commitment to methodological rigor and allow readers to assess the review's robustness, ensuring that the findings stand on a foundation of integrity.

Q. 3: Did the review authors explain their selection of the study designs for inclusion in the review?

Within the intricate tapestry of systematic reviews, the selection of study designs is a critical determinant of the review's comprehensiveness and relevance.

The inclusion and exclusion criteria for primary studies should be clear (We have discussed this topic in detail in Chapter 6).

Q. 4: Did the review authors use a comprehensive literature search strategy?

A comprehensive literature involves forming a wide search across diverse databases, gray literature sources, conference proceedings, and reference lists. Keywords, controlled vocabulary, and Boolean operators are artfully combined to unearth every relevant study pertaining to the research question.

In the context of systematic literature reviews, comprehensive database search is considered as searching in at least four major databases relevant to the subject area.

The details of systematic search could be found in Chapter 5.

Q. 5: Did the review authors perform study selection in duplicate?

In the meticulous process of conducting a systematic review, study selection is akin to curating precious gems, each representing a valuable piece of evidence.

Duplicate study selection stands as a sentinel, guarding the systematic review against individual biases and errors. It involves the independent evaluation of potential studies by at least two researchers. Each study undergoes inspection from multiple lenses, minimizing the risk of overlooking relevant studies or inadvertently including irrelevant ones. This redundancy is not mere repetition; it is a safeguard that ensures the systematic and unbiased inclusion of studies. Please see Chapter 6.

Q. 6: Did the review authors perform data extraction in duplicate?

Authors should extract essential information from selected studies, transforming raw data into structured, usable insights.

Duplicate data extraction (data extraction by two or more independent researchers) elevates the unparalleled precision. This process not only serves as a validation mechanism but also acts as a robust quality control measure. Discrepancies are identified, discussed, and resolved through consensus, ensuring that the extracted data is not influenced by individual biases or oversights. Duplicate extraction enhances the precision and reliability of the review's findings, enhancing its credibility. Please see Chapter 7.

Q. 7: Did the review authors provide a list of excluded studies and justify the exclusions?

The inclusion and exclusion criteria of systematic reviews are the gates through which studies enter or remain outside the review's purview.

Providing a comprehensive list of excluded studies, along with clear justifications for each exclusion, is vital. It allows readers to understand the boundaries set by the review and the criteria used to include or exclude studies. Justifications should be rooted in predetermined criteria, ensuring objectivity. Transparent reporting mitigates potential biases, demonstrating that the review authors' decisions were based on defined parameters rather than subjective judgments.

Q. 8: Did the review authors describe the included studies in adequate detail?

In the grand tapestry of systematic reviews, each included study is a vibrant thread, contributing to the richness of the overall narrative.

Describing included studies in a systematic review is akin to painting a vivid portrait. Each stroke of detail—participant characteristics, intervention nuances, outcomes measured, and methodological intricacies—enhances the study's depth and context. Adequate description is **not** merely a formality; it is the bridge connecting the reader to the essence of the research. A well-described study provides readers with a nuanced understanding of the study's design, execution, and findings.

Q. 9: Did the review authors use a satisfactory technique for assessing the risk of bias (RoB) in individual studies that were included in the review?

RoB assessment is the process of systematically evaluating imperfections, identifying potential sources of bias that could affect a study's internal validity. It is a critical step that allows reviewers and readers to gauge the reliability and credibility of the study findings. A satisfactory RoB assessment method is akin to a magnifying glass, enabling researchers to scrutinize the minutiae of study design and execution.

Satisfactory RoB assessment techniques are those recognized for their validity and reliability. These methods are systematic, transparent, and evidence-based, ensuring consistency across studies. Commonly used tools include the Cochrane Risk of Bias tool for randomized trials (RoB 2.0), the Newcastle–Ottawa Scale for observational studies, Joanna Briggs Institute Critical Appraisal (JBI), and the QUADAS-2 tool for diagnostic accuracy studies. The choice of the RoB assessment tool should align with the study designs included in the systematic review, reflecting the nuances of each research methodology. For more details, see Chapter 8.

Q. 10: Did the review authors report on the sources of funding for the studies included in the review?

Funding sources, whether public institutions, private organizations, or industry entities, play a pivotal role in shaping research agendas. Transparent reporting of these sources is essential for understanding the potential influence on the study outcomes.

The funding source of a study can introduce biases, consciously or unconsciously, influencing the study design, methodology, analysis, and interpretation of results. Acknowledging these potential biases is crucial for readers to critically assess the study's objectivity. Transparent reporting of funding sources allows readers to contextualize the research within the broader landscape, discerning any potential conflicts of interest and biases that might impact the study findings.

Q. 11: If meta-analysis was performed did the review authors use appropriate methods for statistical combination of results?

Within the symphony of systematic reviews, meta-analysis is the harmonious fusion of individual study findings, creating a powerful crescendo of evidence. The 11th question in AMSTAR-2 delves into this intricate aspect, asking: "If meta-analysis was performed, did the review authors use appropriate methods for the statistical combination of results?"

For readers, awareness of appropriate meta-analysis methods is akin to discerning musical notes within a symphony.

For researchers, using appropriate methods in meta-analysis is a testament to methodological excellence. By employing robust statistical techniques, researchers uphold the integrity of their synthesis, ensuring that the meta-analysis stands as a pinnacle of evidence-based knowledge (See Chapter 9 &10).

Q. 12: If meta-analysis was performed, did the review authors assess the potential impact of RoB in individual studies on the results of the meta-analysis or other evidence synthesis?

The potential impact of bias on meta-analysis is a an important issue, if not carefully examined, might distort the entire fabric of evidence synthesis.

Bias, like a subtle shadow, can cast an imperceptible veil over study results, affecting the integrity of meta-analytical findings. Assessing the potential impact of bias in individual studies is paramount, as it allows researchers to gauge the reliability of the synthesized evidence. Recognizing and addressing bias ensures that the conclusions drawn from meta-analysis are robust, trustworthy, and free from undue influence. biases in systematic reviews can stem from a variety of sources, including methodological differences among the included studies and statistical variations. While subgroup analysis can help mitigate certain types of heterogeneity, there are still factors that persist and need to be acknowledged in the discussion section of the review. The address of this item in meta-analysis is important.

Q. 13: Did the review authors account for RoB in individual studies when interpreting/discussing the results of the review?

In the intricate process of systematic review, the potential influence of risk of bias (RoB) on the interpretation of findings is akin to viewing the world through a prism.

RoB, whether subtle or pronounced, can cast its shadow on the review's interpretation. Accounting for RoB is critical because it allows reviewers to assess the reliability of the evidence and its potential limitations. Each study's RoB profile should be considered when discussing the results, as the level of confidence in the findings is intricately linked to the methodological quality of the included studies (see Chapter 8).

Q. 14: Did the review authors provide a satisfactory explanation for, and discussion of, any heterogeneity observed in the results of the review?

Within the diverse landscape of systematic reviews, the presence of heterogeneity is akin to navigating uncharted territories.

For readers, a satisfactory explanation of heterogeneity is akin to having a compass guiding them through diverse terrains.

For researchers, providing a satisfactory explanation for heterogeneity is a testament to methodological rigor. By delving into the intricacies of heterogeneity, researchers uphold the standards of excellence, ensuring that the systematic review is not just a synthesis of data points but a comprehensive exploration of the evidence landscape.

Evaluating the heterogeneity between the results of the included studies, and finding the source in the meta-analysis will help better interpretation of the results and paying attention to the source of heterogeneity (see Chapter 13).

Q. 15: If they performed quantitative synthesis did the review authors carry out an adequate investigation of publication bias (small study bias) and discuss its likely impact on the results of the review?

Publication bias, the tendency for studies with positive or significant results to be published, while studies with negative or nonsignificant results remain unpublished, is a subtle yet pervasive influence. It skews the available evidence, painting an incomplete and potentially misleading picture. Quantitative synthesis, when not mindful of publication bias, might inadvertently magnify this distortion.

Adequate investigation of publication bias involves employing various techniques, such as funnel plots, Egger's regression test, or trim-and-fill analysis. These methods scrutinize the symmetry of the data distribution, identifying potential biases introduced by unpublished or missing studies. Thorough exploration is essential to comprehend the impact of publication bias on the review's findings. It enables reviewers to assess the robustness of the evidence and acknowledge the potential limitations introduced by this bias (see Chapter 12).

Q. 16: Did the review authors report any potential sources of conflict of interest, including any funding they received for conducting the review?

Full disclosure of potential conflicts of interest is foundational to maintaining the integrity and credibility of a systematic review. Conflicts of interest can arise from various sources, such as financial ties to pharmaceutical companies, industry affiliations, or personal beliefs. Acknowledging these potential biases allows readers to assess the review's objectivity and interpret the findings within a transparent context.

The need for openness and honesty

Review authors must provide a clear account of any financial or nonfinancial interests that could influence their judgment or the review process. This transparency enables readers to critically evaluate the review's conclusions and consider the potential impact of author affiliations or funding sources. Openness and honesty in disclosing conflicts of interest foster trust between researchers and readers, ensuring that the review's findings are viewed through an unbiased lens.

Empowering readers with critical awareness

For readers, awareness of potential conflicts of interest empowers them to approach the review's findings with critical awareness. Understanding the affiliations and interests of the review authors allows readers to contextualize the conclusions and make well-informed judgments. Informed readership ensures that the evidence is evaluated within a framework of transparency, enabling readers to weigh the review's credibility against potential biases.

Upholding the standards of ethical conduct

For researchers, reporting potential conflicts of interest is not just a formality; it is a commitment to ethical conduct. By openly acknowledging affiliations, funding sources, or personal interests, researchers uphold the standards of integrity and accountability. Transparent reporting of conflicts of interest reflects a dedication to unbiased inquiry, ensuring that the systematic review stands as an exemplar of ethical research practices.

Finally, the maintenance of transparency in the review process serves as a fundamental pillar upholding the integrity of scholarly research. It not only acts as a safeguard against bias and manipulation but also cultivates a culture of trust among researchers and readers alike. This commitment to transparency ensures that the synthesis of evidence remains firmly rooted in principles of honesty, openness, and an unyielding dedication to the pursuit of objective truth. Such ethical practices are essential in promoting the credibility and reliability of academic discourse, fostering an environment where knowledge can be rigorously examined and built upon with confidence.

Reference

[1]   Shea BJ, Grimshaw JM, Wellhs GA, Boers M, Andersson N, Hamel C, et al. Development of AMSTAR: a measurement tool to assess the methodological quality of systematic reviews. BMC Med Res Methodol 2007;7:1−7.

Scientific writing in a systematic review and Meta-Analyses

17

Paria Dehesh

Kerman University of Medical Science, Department of Biostatistic and Epidemiology, Kerman, Iran

Systematic studies and meta-analyses are very important for healthcare providers, policymakers, and other decision-makers because they make decisions more accurately by combining the results of a large amount of research. For decision-makers to assess the reliability of systematic results, the results of systematic studies should be clear to allow others apply the results confidently. The Preferred Reporting Items for Systematic Reviews and Meta-Analyses (PRISMA) [1] Statement, published in 2009 [2], is designed to help authors prepare clear reports of their studies [3]. It has been updated in 2020 [4].

PRISMA is a reporting guide, which is designed to help authors to address reporting of systematic reviews [5]. PRISMA 2020 includes 27 items and could be applied for original or updates systematic reviews [4] (Figs. 17.1 and 17.2).

Being familiar with PRISMA guideline before conducting the systematic review will help you to ensure that all steps are done perfectly and all recommended information is captured [6].

Publishers and journals have the right to set word counts, section counts, and maximum numbers of tables and figures that can be included in the main article [6]. When this happens, it might be enough just to cite the protocol in the main article if the information is already publicly available. Additionally, extra results or more details on the procedures employed can be added and sent to the journals as supplemental files. The description of the various sections of the systematic report and meta-analysis writing process will be covered in the following.

To make systematic review article easier to access for potential users, it would be better to include the words "systematic review and meta-analysis" in the title. It is not recommended to use terms "review," "literature review," "evidence synthesis," or "knowledge synthesis" since they fail to distinguish between systematic reviews and nonsystematic reviews [7]. Furthermore, the terms "meta-analysis" and "systematic review" should not be used interchangeably in the title because the latter only refers to statistical synthesis and the former refers to the full set of procedures used to find, pick, and synthesize evidence. Important details regarding the primary goal or query that the review is meant to answer should be included in the title (e.g., type of interventions, target population, and type of studies included in the review) (Fig. 17.3).

Systematic Review and Meta-Analysis. **https://doi.org/10.1016/B978-0-443-13428-9.00017-3**

Section and Topic	Item #	Checklist item	Location where item is reported
TITLE			
Title	1	Identify the report as a systematic review.	
ABSTRACT			
Abstract	2	See the PRISMA 2020 for Abstracts checklist.	
INTRODUCTION			
Rationale	3	Describe the rationale for the review in the context of existing knowledge.	
Objectives	4	Provide an explicit statement of the objective(s) or question(s) the review addresses.	
METHODS			
Eligibility criteria	5	Specify the inclusion and exclusion criteria for the review and how studies were grouped for the syntheses.	
Information sources	6	Specify all databases, registers, websites, organisations, reference lists and other sources searched or consulted to identify studies. Specify the date when each source was last searched or consulted.	
Search strategy	7	Present the full search strategies for all databases, registers and websites, including any filters and limits used.	
Selection process	8	Specify the methods used to decide whether a study met the inclusion criteria of the review, including how many reviewers screened each record and each report retrieved, whether they worked independently, and if applicable, details of automation tools used in the process.	
Data collection process	9	Specify the methods used to collect data from reports, including how many reviewers collected data from each report, whether they worked independently, any processes for obtaining or confirming data from study investigators, and if applicable, details of automation tools used in the process.	
Data items	10a	List and define all outcomes for which data were sought. Specify whether all results that were compatible with each outcome domain in each study were sought (e.g. for all measures, time points, analyses), and if not, the methods used to decide which results to collect.	
	10b	List and define all other variables for which data were sought (e.g. participant and intervention characteristics, funding sources). Describe any assumptions made about any missing or unclear information.	
Study risk of bias assessment	11	Specify the methods used to assess risk of bias in the included studies, including details of the tool(s) used, how many reviewers assessed each study and whether they worked independently, and if applicable, details of automation tools used in the process.	
Effect measures	12	Specify for each outcome the effect measure(s) (e.g. risk ratio, mean difference) used in the synthesis or presentation of results.	
Synthesis methods	13a	Describe the processes used to decide which studies were eligible for each synthesis (e.g. tabulating the study intervention characteristics and comparing against the planned groups for each synthesis (item #5)).	
	13b	Describe any methods required to prepare the data for presentation or synthesis, such as handling of missing summary statistics, or data conversions.	
	13c	Describe any methods used to tabulate or visually display results of individual studies and syntheses.	
	13d	Describe any methods used to synthesize results and provide a rationale for the choice(s). If meta-analysis was performed, describe the model(s), method(s) to identify the presence and extent of statistical heterogeneity, and software package(s) used.	
	13e	Describe any methods used to explore possible causes of heterogeneity among study results (e.g. subgroup analysis, meta-regression).	
	13f	Describe any sensitivity analyses conducted to assess robustness of the synthesized results.	
Reporting bias assessment	14	Describe any methods used to assess risk of bias due to missing results in a synthesis (arising from reporting biases).	

FIGURE 17.1

The first page of PRISMA 2020.

Section and Topic	Item #	Checklist item	Location where item is reported
Certainty assessment	15	Describe any methods used to assess certainty (or confidence) in the body of evidence for an outcome.	
RESULTS			
Study selection	16a	Describe the results of the search and selection process, from the number of records identified in the search to the number of studies included in the review, ideally using a flow diagram.	
	16b	Cite studies that might appear to meet the inclusion criteria, but which were excluded, and explain why they were excluded.	
Study characteristics	17	Cite each included study and present its characteristics.	
Risk of bias in studies	18	Present assessments of risk of bias for each included study.	
Results of individual studies	19	For all outcomes, present, for each study: (a) summary statistics for each group (where appropriate) and (b) an effect estimate and its precision (e.g. confidence/credible interval), ideally using structured tables or plots.	
Results of syntheses	20a	For each synthesis, briefly summarise the characteristics and risk of bias among contributing studies.	
	20b	Present results of all statistical syntheses conducted. If meta-analysis was done, present for each the summary estimate and its precision (e.g. confidence/credible interval) and measures of statistical heterogeneity. If comparing groups, describe the direction of the effect.	
	20c	Present results of all investigations of possible causes of heterogeneity among study results.	
	20d	Present results of all sensitivity analyses conducted to assess the robustness of the synthesized results.	
Reporting biases	21	Present assessments of risk of bias due to missing results (arising from reporting biases) for each synthesis assessed.	
Certainty of evidence	22	Present assessments of certainty (or confidence) in the body of evidence for each outcome assessed.	
DISCUSSION			
Discussion	23a	Provide a general interpretation of the results in the context of other evidence.	
	23b	Discuss any limitations of the evidence included in the review.	
	23c	Discuss any limitations of the review processes used.	
	23d	Discuss implications of the results for practice, policy, and future research.	
OTHER INFORMATION			
Registration and protocol	24a	Provide registration information for the review, including register name and registration number, or state that the review was not registered.	
	24b	Indicate where the review protocol can be accessed, or state that a protocol was not prepared.	
	24c	Describe and explain any amendments to information provided at registration or in the protocol.	
Support	25	Describe sources of financial or non-financial support for the review, and the role of the funders or sponsors in the review.	
Competing interests	26	Declare any competing interests of review authors.	
Availability of data, code and other materials	27	Report which of the following are publicly available and where they can be found: template data collection forms; data extracted from included studies; data used for all analyses; analytic code; any other materials used in the review.	

FIGURE 17.2

The second page of PRISMA 2020.

From: Page MJ, McKenzie JE, Bossuyt PM, Boutron I, Hoffmann TC, Mulrow CD, Shamseer L, Tetzlaff JM, Akl EA, Brennan SE, Chou R, Glanville J, Grimshaw JM, Hróbjartsson A, Lalu MM, Li T, Loder EW, Mayo-Wilson E, McDonald S, McGuinness LA, Stewart LA, Thomas J, Tricco AC, Welch VA, Whiting P, Moher D. The PRISMA 2020 statement: an updated guideline for reporting systematic reviews. Int J Surg 2021;88(1). https://doi.org/10.1016/j.ijsu.2021.105906.

PRISMA 2020 for Abstracts Checklist

Section and Topic	Item #	Checklist item	Reported (Yes/No)
TITLE			
Title	1	Identify the report as a systematic review.	
BACKGROUND			
Objectives	2	Provide an explicit statement of the main objective(s) or question(s) the review addresses.	
METHODS			
Eligibility criteria	3	Specify the inclusion and exclusion criteria for the review.	
Information sources	4	Specify the information sources (e.g. databases, registers) used to identify studies and the date when each was last searched.	
Risk of bias	5	Specify the methods used to assess risk of bias in the included studies.	
Synthesis of results	6	Specify the methods used to present and synthesise results.	
RESULTS			
Included studies	7	Give the total number of included studies and participants and summarise relevant characteristics of studies.	
Synthesis of results	8	Present results for main outcomes, preferably indicating the number of included studies and participants for each. If meta-analysis was done, report the summary estimate and confidence/credible interval. If comparing groups, indicate the direction of the effect (i.e. which group is favoured).	
DISCUSSION			
Limitations of evidence	9	Provide a brief summary of the limitations of the evidence included in the review (e.g. study risk of bias, inconsistency and imprecision).	
Interpretation	10	Provide a general interpretation of the results and important implications.	
OTHER			
Funding	11	Specify the primary source of funding for the review.	
Registration	12	Provide the register name and registration number.	

FIGURE 17.3

PRISMA 2020 abstract guideline.

From: Page MJ, McKenzie JE, Bossuyt PM, Boutron I, Hoffmann TC, Mulrow CD, Shamseer L, Tetzlaff JM, Akl FA, Brennan SE, Chou R, Glanville J, Grimshaw JM, Hróbjartsson A, Lalu MM, Li T, Loder EW, Mayo-Wilson E, McDonald S, McGuinness LA, Stewart LA, Thomas J, Tricco AC, Welch VA, Whiting P, Moher D. The PRISMA 2020 statement: an updated guideline for reporting systematic reviews. Int J Surg 2021;88(1). https://doi.org/ 10.1016/j.ijsu.2021.105906.

Part of your document could not be imported as it contained an unsupported element. For more information about unsupported elements, please visit the Support Center.

Introduction
Rational

The introduction section of a systematic review serves to provide readers with an understanding of the purpose and significance of the study. It begins by presenting the current state of knowledge and any uncertainties or gaps in existing literature. This sets the stage for explaining the importance of conducting a systematic review. If there are previous systematic reviews that have addressed a similar question, it is necessary to explain why the current review is still crucial. This could be due to old information in the previous reviews, the use of new methods to address the research question, or the presence of methodological problems in existing studies. By highlighting these factors, the introduction establishes the rationale for conducting a new systematic review. If the objective of the systematic review is to update an available systematic review, it is important to mention in the introduction that the current study aims to provide an updated analysis. Additionally, if the systematic review includes studies on intervention effects, it is beneficial to provide a brief explanation of the underlying mechanisms or theories that may explain how the interventions work.

Objectives

If the objective is to assess the effects of interventions, the PICO framework (Population, Intervention, Comparison, Outcome) or one of its variations can be applied. This framework helps to clearly define the population under study, the interventions being investigated, the comparisons, and the outcomes of interest. Using the PICO framework or a similar approach enhances the clarity and precision of the study's objectives or questions.

Methods
Eligibility criteria

Inclusion criteria: Specifying the criteria that are used to decide eligible articles for including in the systematic review should be provided in sufficient detail.

Eligibility criteria should be clear, and reproducible.

All inclusion criteria based on PICO should be clearly defined, such as studies using specific criteria for recruitment, specific duration of follow-up.

It is crucial to clearly state the exclusion criteria such as language limitations, studies type except what you desire to include:

Information resources

All databases, webpages, reference lists, and other sources that are used to find studies must be listed in this section. Specify the date of search for each database. The "what, when, and how" of sources and databases should be fully reported by authors to enable future updates of this systematic review.

It is best to list the name of each database (MEDLINE, SCOPUS, etc.) along with the platform or interface that was used (Ovid, for example). The names of each source and any previous restrictions imposed were noted as we searched regulatory databases (such as Drugs@ FDA), online repositories (such as the SIDER side effects resource), and clinical trial study registries (such as ClinicalTrials.gov). Indicate each resource's URL.

Search strategy

To increase the systematic review's transparency and replicability, all search strategy details—should be included in this section.

Details of the methods used to find keywords, synonyms, or subject indexing terms used in the search strategies or any process might be provided in this section.

For example, MeSH terms that were used in PubMed and the final search strategy should be provided in details.

Selection process: Studies are often chosen for inclusion in a systematic review using a multistep process that starts with title screening, followed by abstracts assessment, full text evaluation, and finally ends with an extraction of desired information.

The number of each stage and their initials as well as disagreement solution method should be clearly stated. If researchers who screened abstracts are different from who screened the full texts, it should be clarified.

You must specify the translation process used if abstracts or articles need to be translated into another language to be included in the systematization. It is necessary to report the number of articles targeted during screening in the PRISMA diagram.

Data collection process

Describe the methods used to collect data from the eligible articles, including how many authors collected data from each article, and whether they worked independently or not. Also, mention what process was used to resolve disagreements between data collectors. If the articles needed to be translated into another language for data collection, report how these articles were translated. If the software was used to extract data from the figures, specify the applied software [8].

Data items

The writers of systematic reviews may choose to use particular outcomes or extract all outcomes.

Researchers should clearly define the outcomes of interest and extract them carefully from included studies. They should consider the units, time intervals, report type (as a categorical or continuous variable), etc. [9].

For each study, bibliographic data such as name of the first author, publication year, country of origin, if needed, name of the journal, and sample characteristics such as size, recruitment criteria, and demographic characteristics such as mean age, sex ratio, disease duration, stage or grade of the disease, and medications, especially the main outcomes should be extracted [10].

Assessing the risk of bias

In this section, you should describe the tool that you applied for risk of bias assessment of included studies (tools are described in details in Chapter 8).

Also, you should report how many reviewers evaluated each study and if they worked independently. Mention what they did when they had disagreement [11].

You can exclude low-quality studies from meta-analysis and described the reason of omission in the result section of the manuscript. Low-quality manuscripts (biased results) may distort the final results of the systematic review and meta-analysis [12].

Effect measures

The authors may decide to express the findings using different effect measures.

Therefore, the effect measure(s) (such as risk ratio and mean difference) used for combining the data should be defined for each outcome For categorical variables define if you applied odds ratio, risk difference or risk ratio to pool data. For continuous variables define if you want to pool means, mean difference (MDs), standardized mean difference (SMDs), etc. [13].

Also, you can define if you want to pool incidences or prevalences excluded from included studies.

Data synthesis methods

In this section, you have to explain the process you applied for including studies in systematic review/meta-analysis. Provide details regarding excluding retrieved studies, and the reason.

You have to describe if you prepared the data for presentation or synthesis in your systematic review or not, such as handling of missing data, converting data (for example calculating BMI based on weight, and height), changing the unit from kg to gram, etc.) [14].

The graphical method that is applied for visualization of results, such as forest plots and funnel plots, should be explained in this part [15].

In this section, you will report the software you used for synthesis, model of pooling the results (random vs. fixed), method of reporting heterogeneity (Cochran's Q, Tau^2, I^2), how you dealt with the possible causes of heterogeneity (subgroup analysis, meta-regression), and if you did sensitivity analysis, etc. [16].

If your systematic review includes meta-analysis, this part is very important and plays crucial role in the manuscript acceptance [16].

Bias assessment report: The validity of the meta-analysis may be distorted when the available results differ systematically from those of the missing studies. This is known as 'bias due to missing results' and arises from 'reporting biases' such as selective nondisclosure and selective under-reporting results. Statistical and graphical methods are available to assess whether observed data represent the potential for missing results (such as contour-enhanced funnel plots, and Egger's test) [17].

Determine how many authors assessed the risk of bias due to missing results in a cohort, whether multiple authors worked independently, and what process was used to resolve disagreements [18]. Report any processes used to obtain or verify relevant information from study investigators.

Assess certainty: Authors typically utilize certain criteria to make determinations regarding their level of confidence (or certainty) in the evidence presented for each significant outcome [19].

Results
Study selection

To help readers understand the progression of retrieved records up to inclusion in the review, authors of review articles should ideally use a flowchart to report the results of the search and selection process. Information specialists can use this information to assess their search tactics. Others can better understand the search's process by knowing how many records were retrieved from each database, how many duplicates were deleted, and how many full texts were evaluated [19].

The following elements can be illustrated within a flowchart: records that were excluded before screening (duplication, failure to meet criteria, etc.); records that were screened; records that were excluded following title or title/abstract screening; records that were retrieved for full-text evaluation; records that were retrieved but did not meet the inclusion criteria (e.g., inappropriate study design, inappropriate population); and the total number of studies and records included in the review [20].

The identification of excluded records allows readers to assess the credibility and applicability of the systematic review. These details can be reported in the text in the form of a list/table within the report or in an online supplement. Potential controversial exceptions should be clearly stated in the report.

Characteristics of the study

For each included study, summarize excluded data and its characteristics, in a table. In most systematic reviews, the first table is designed to show basic characteristics and main findings.

Risk of bias in studies: It is important to provide information regarding the risk of bias of included studies to assist readers understand the internal validity of the results of a systematic review. It is insufficient to report summary data alone (e.g., "two out of eight studies successfully blinded participants") as this does not tell readers which particular studies contained a particular methodological flaw [21]. To help users understand which factors contribute to the overall risk of bias at the study level, it is more informative to provide tables or figures that indicate the risk of bias assessed for each study in each domain/component/assessment item (e.g., blinding in randomized controlled trials or loss of outcome data). If the risk of bias assessment has been conducted for specific outcomes or results in each study, consider displaying the risk of bias judgments in a forest plot alongside the study results. This allows the limitations of the studies that contribute to a particular meta-analysis to be evident [22].

Results of individual studies

For all outcomes, ideally, provide (a) summary statistics for each group (if applicable) and (b) an effect estimate and its precision (such as confidence interval/credibility interval) for each study. It is recommended to present this information using structured tables or graphical displays. Presenting data from individual studies allows understanding of individual study findings and their proportion in meta-analysis [23].

There are various methods for presenting the results of individual studies (such as tables and forest plots). Visual representation of the results supports interpretation by readers while tabulating the results makes data reuse easier for others [24].

Results of syntheses: If a meta-analysis has been carried out, each one's measurements and summary estimates together with their precision—such as the confidence intervals—must be disclosed. For each synthesis, briefly summarize the characteristics of each individual study and report the risk of bias among contributing studies [25].

In systematic reviews including meta-analysis, report the summary estimate for outcomes of interest and also precision such as confidence/credible intervals [26].

For each outcome of interest that you estimated pooled effect, report heterogeneity findings such as Cochran's Q, I^2, and Tau^2. If you did subgroup analysis or meta-regression, report all of them.

When comparing different groups, report the direction of the effects based on the pooled estimate.

If you did sensitivity analysis, report all steps and results in this part of your paper.

Report of bias in synthesis

In this section, you should report the risk of bias due to missing results for each synthesis assessed.

If a tool has been used to assess the risk of reporting bias due to missing results in a particular combination, provide answers to the questions included in the tool, judgments about the risk of bias, and any supporting information used to justify those judgments. If a funnel plot has been created to assess small study effects (one of the reasons being reporting biases), present the plot and indicate the effect estimate and measure of precision, which is used in the plot (typically presented on the horizontal and vertical axes) [27].

- If a test for funnel plot asymmetry has been used, report the exact observed *P*-value for the test and other relevant statistics, such as the standardized normal deviation,
- If any sensitivity analysis has been conducted to examine the potential impact of missing results on the synthesis, present the results of each analysis and compare them with the initial analysis,
- If the assessment of selective outcome report indicates that some studies are missing from the combination, consider representing those studies as missing results as a subgroup in a forest plot or add a table including missing results.

Certainty of evidence

To report certainty level of your evidence, you can use Grading of Recommendations Assessment, Development, and Evaluation (GRADE) to help readers become aware of the validity and reliability of your evidence [28].

Based on GRADE, we can categorize evidences into the following (n.d.):

Very low	The true effect is probably markedly different from the estimated effect
Low	The true effect might be markedly different from the estimated effect
Moderate	The authors believe that the true effect is probably close to the estimated effect
High	The authors have a lot of confidence that the true effect is similar to the estimated effect

Factors that affect certainty of the evidence are (n.d.):

1. Risk of bias: GRADE evaluates the level of the evidence at outcome level not in study level.
   Studies with high level of bias present higher level of uncertainty for presented outcome (details of risk of bias could be found in Chapter 8).
2. Imprecision: GRADE approach focuses on confidence interval level for the estimate [29]. The imprecision will rise if the pooled effect comes from small studies (details could be found in Chapter 10).
3. Inconsistency: Heterogeneity between results of included studies may raise uncertainty of pooled estimate (details could be found in Chapter 13).
4. Indirectness: When external validity of the evidence is low due to difference in study population and whom the evidence is applied or when the studies interventions are not applicable in real world.
5. Publication bias: The most important factor that affects certainty of the evidence is publication bias, which is discussed in details in Chapter 12.

Discussion

In this section you should provide a general interpretation of your results, their confidence intervals and their application in the practice.

You also could compare your results with previous systematic reviews/meta-analyses and discuss some included original studies.

The discussion section should address any limitations encountered during the review process. It should provide clear understanding of the comprehensiveness, relevance, and level of uncertainty associated with the evidence, which is presented in the review, and enables them to accurately interpret the findings. To illustrate this, authors may acknowledge that the review was based on a limited number of studies or studies with small sample sizes, resulting in imprecise estimates. They may also address concerns regarding potential bias in the included studies, and missing data [30].

In this section, authors should discuss implications of the results for various audiences.

Patients and healthcare providers may primarily focus on assessing the balance between the benefits and harms of the intervention, while policymakers may consider data on organizational impact and resource utilization. When examining interventions, authors may clarify the trade-off between benefits and harms [31].

In addition, rather than offering suggestions for globally applicable actions or policies, authors could talk about elements that are crucial in converting evidence into practice or policy.

Other information

Registration and protocol:

Give details on the registration of the protocol, such as the name of the website and registration number, or whether the protocol is not registered.

Modifications to the protocol should be explained in details. Any changes made to the data entered at registration or in the protocol must be clearly stated and justified [32].

Support

Explain source of financial and nonfinancial support, as well as the sponsors' and funders' roles in the systematic review.

Clarify the role of funders in supporting software, payment to authors, etc. [33].

Competing interests

Clarify if there is any relationship between authors and financial supporters or if any industry supported the studies.

Describe if you used other data and the permission process or if you asked authors to send you original data of their manuscript [34].

Availability of data, code and other materials:

You should provide related data, data collection form that is used for data gathering, data that were used for meta-analysis, analytic code, and other material, which were used in your review [35].

References

[1] Liberati A, Altman DG, Tetzlaff J, et al. The PRISMA statement for reporting systematic reviews and meta-analyses of studies that evaluate health care interventions: explanation and elaboration. J Clin Epidemiol 2009;62:e1—34. https://doi.org/10.1016/j.jclinepi.2009.06.006.

[2] Moher D, Liberati A, Tetzlaff J, Altman DG. Preferred reporting items for systematic reviews and meta-analyses: the PRISMA statement. BMJ 2009;339:b2535. https://doi.org/10.1136/bmj.b2535.

[3] Takkouche B, Norman G. PRISMA statement. Epidemiology 2011;22(1). https://doi.org/10.1097/ede.0b013e3181fe7999.

[4] Page MJ, McKenzie JE, Bossuyt PM, Boutron I, Hoffmann TC, Mulrow CD, Shamseer L, Tetzlaff JM, Akl EA, Brennan SE, Chou R, Glanville J, Grimshaw JM, Hróbjartsson A, Lalu MM, Li T, Loder EW, Mayo-Wilson E, McDonald S, McGuinness LA, Stewart LA, Thomas J, Tricco AC, Welch VA, Whiting P, Moher D. The PRISMA 2020 statement: an updated guideline for reporting systematic reviews. Int J Surg 2021;88(1). https://doi.org/10.1016/j.ijsu.2021.105906.

[5] Moher D, Tetzlaff J, Tricco AC, Sampson M, Altman DG. Epidemiology and reporting characteristics of systematic reviews. PLoS Med 2007;4(3):447—55. https://doi.org/10.1371/journal.pmed.0040078.

[6] Liberati A, Altman DG, Tetzlaff J, et al. The PRISMA statement for reporting systematic reviews and meta-analyses of studies that evaluate health care interventions: explanation and elaboration. PLoS Med 2009;6:e1000100. https://doi.org/10.1371/journal.pmed.1000100.

[7] Page MJ, Moher D. Evaluations of the uptake and impact of the preferred reporting items for systematic reviews and meta-analyses (PRISMA) statement and extensions: a scoping review. Syst Rev 2017;6:263. https://doi.org/10.1186/s13643-017-0663-8.

[8] Moher D, Shamseer L, Clarke M, et al. Preferred reporting items for systematic review and meta-analysis protocols (PRISMA-P) 2015 statement. Syst Rev 2015;4:1. https://doi.org/10.1186/2046-4053-4-1.

[9] Shamseer L, Moher D, Clarke M, et al. Preferred reporting items for systematic review and meta-analysis protocols (PRISMA-P) 2015: elaboration and explanation. BMJ 2015;350:g7647. https://doi.org/10.1136/bmj.g7647.

[10] Page MJ, McKenzie JE, Bossuyt PM, et al. The PRISMA 2020 statement: an updated guideline for reporting systematic reviews. BMJ 2021;372:n71. https://doi.org/10.1136/bmj.n71.

[11] Page MJ, McKenzie JE, Bossuyt PM, et al. Updating guidance for reporting systematic reviews: development of the PRISMA 2020 statement. J Clin Epidemiol 2021. https://doi.org/10.1016/j.jclinepi.2021.02.003. S0895-4356(21)00040-8.

[12] Tong A, Flemming K, McInnes E, Oliver S, Craig J. Enhancing transparency in reporting the synthesis of qualitative research. ENTREQ. BMC Med Res Methodol 2012;12: 181. https://doi.org/10.1186/1471-2288-12-181.

[13] Barnes C, Boutron I, Giraudeau B, Porcher R, Altman DG, Ravaud P. Impact of an online writing aid tool for writing a randomized trial report: the COBWEB (Consort-based WEB tool) randomized controlled trial. BMC Med 2015;13:221. https://doi.org/10.1186/s12916-015-0460-y.

[14] Chauvin A, Ravaud P, Moher D, et al. Accuracy in detecting inadequate research reporting by early career peer reviewers using an online CONSORT-based peer-review tool (COBPeer) versus the usual peer-review process: a cross-sectional diagnostic study. BMC Med 2019;17:205. https://doi.org/10.1186/s12916-019-1436-0.

[15] Higgins JPT, Thomas J, Chandler J, et al., editors. Cochrane handbook for systematic reviews of interventions. Cochrane Collaboration; 2019. Version 6.0. https://training.cochrane.org/handbook.

[16] McKenzie JE, Brennan SE. Synthesizing and presenting findings using other methods. In: Higgins JPT, Thomas J, Chandler J, ct al., editors. Cochrane Handbook for Systematic Reviews of Interventions. Cochrane Collaboration; 2019. https://doi.org/10.1002/9781119536604.ch12.

[17] Beller EM, Glasziou PP, Altman DG, et al., PRISMA for Abstracts Group. PRISMA for Abstracts: reporting systematic reviews in journal and conference abstracts. PLoS Med 2013;10:e1001419. https://doi.org/10.1371/journal.pmed.1001419.

[18] France EF, Cunningham M, Ring N, et al. Improving reporting of meta-ethnography: the eMERGe reporting guidance. BMC Med Res Methodol 2019;19:25. https://doi.org/10.1186/s12874-018-0600-0.

[19] Welch V, Petticrew M, Petkovic J, et al. PRISMA-Equity Bellagio group. Extending the PRISMA statement to equity-focused systematic reviews (PRISMA-E 2012): explanation and elaboration. J Clin Epidemiol 2016;70:68—89. https://doi.org/10.1016/j.jclinepi.2015.09.001.

[20] Hutton B, Salanti G, Caldwell DM, et al. The PRISMA extension statement for reporting of systematic reviews incorporating network meta-analyses of health care interventions: checklist and explanations. Ann Intern Med 2015;162:777—84. https://doi.org/10.7326/M14-2385.

[21] Thomas J, Kneale D, McKenzie JE. Determining the scope of the review and the questions it will address. In: Higgins JPT, Thomas J, Chandler J, et al., editors. Cochrane Handbook for Systematic Reviews of Interventions. Cochrane Collaboration; 2019. https://doi.org/10.1002/9781119536604.ch2.

[22] Stewart LA, Clarke M, Rovers M, et al. PRISMA-IPD Development Group. Preferred reporting items for systematic review and meta- analyses of individual participant data: the PRISMA-IPD statement. JAMA 2015;313:1657—65. https://doi.org/10.1001/jama.2015.3656.

[23] Rehfuess EA, Booth A, Brereton L, et al. Towards a taxonomy of logic models in systematic reviews and health technology assessments: a priori, staged, and iterative approaches. Res Synth Methods 2018;9:13—24. https://doi.org/10.1002/jrsm.1254.

[24] Zorzela L, Loke YK, Ioannidis JP, et al. PRISMA harms checklist: improving harms reporting in systematic reviews. BMJ 2016;352:i157. https://doi.org/10.1136/bmj.i157.

[25] Booth A, Noyes J, Flemming K, Moore G, Tunçalp Ö, Shakibazadeh E. Formulating questions to explore complex interventions within qualitative evidence synthesis. BMJ Glob Health 2019;4(Suppl. 1):e001107. https://doi.org/10.1136/bmjgh-2018-001107.

[26] Munn Z, Stern C, Aromataris E, Lockwood C, Jordan Z. What kind of systematic review should I conduct? A proposed typology and guidance for systematic reviewers in the medical and health sciences. BMC Med Res Methodol 2018;18:5. https://doi.org/10.1186/s12874-017-0468-4.

[27] McInnes MDF, Moher D, Thombs BD, et al., PRISMA-DTA Group. Preferred reporting items for a systematic review and meta-analysis of diagnostic test accuracy studies: the PRISMA-DTA statement. JAMA 2018;319:388—96. https://doi.org/10.1001/jama.2017.19163.

[28] Yousefifard M, Shafiee A. Should the reporting certainty of evidence for meta-analysis of observational studies using GRADE be revisited? Int J Surg 2023;109(2):129—30. https://doi.org/10.1097/js9.0000000000000114.

[29] Guyatt GH, Oxman AD, Kunz R, Brozek J, Alonso-Coello P, Rind D, Devereaux PJ, Montori VM, Freyschuss B, Vist G, Jaeschke R, Williams JW, Murad MH, Sinclair D, Falck-Ytter Y, Meerpohl J, Whittington C, Thorlund K, Andrews J, Schünemann HJ. GRADE guidelines 6. Rating the quality of evidence - imprecision. J Clin Epidemiol 2011;64(12):1283—93. https://doi.org/10.1016/j.jclinepi.2011.01.012.

[30] IOM Institute of Medicine. Finding what works in health care: standards for systematic reviews. The National Academies Press; 2011.

[31] Page MJ, Shamseer L, Altman DG, et al. Epidemiology and reporting characteristics of systematic reviews of biomedical research: a cross-sectional study. PLoS Med 2016;13: e1002028. https://doi.org/10.1371/journal.pmed.1002028.

[32] McKenzie JE, Brennan SE, Ryan RE, et al. Defining the criteria for including studies and how they will be grouped for the synthesis. In: Higgins JPT, Thomas J, Chandler J, et al., editors. Cochrane Handbook for Systematic Reviews of Interventions. Cochrane Collaboration; 2019. https://doi.org/10.1002/9781119536604.ch3.

[33] Chamberlain C, O'Mara-Eves A, Porter J, et al. Psychosocial interventions for supporting women to stop smoking in pregnancy. Cochrane Database Syst Rev 2017;2: CD001055. https://doi.org/10.1002/14651858.CD001055.pub5.

[34] Dwan KM, Williamson PR, Kirkham JJ. Do systematic reviews still exclude studies with "no relevant outcome data"? BMJ 2017;358:j3919. https://doi.org/10.1136/bmj.j3919.

[35] Lefebvre C, Glanville J, Briscoe S, et al. Searching for and selecting studies. In: Higgins JPT, Thomas J, Chandler J, et al., editors. Cochrane Handbook for Systematic Reviews of Interventions. Cochrane Collaboration; 2019. https://doi.org/10.1002/9781119536604.ch4.

Further reading

[1] Moher D, Liberati A, Tetzlaff J, Altman DG, PRISMA Group. Reprint–preferred reporting items for systematic reviews and meta-analyses: the PRISMA statement. Phys Ther 2009;89:873—80. https://doi.org/10.1093/ptj/89.9.873.

[2] Liberati A, Altman DG, Tetzlaff J, et al. The PRISMA statement for reporting systematic reviews and meta-analyses of studies that evaluate healthcare interventions: explanation and elaboration. BMJ 2009;339:b2700. https://doi.org/10.1136/bmj.b2700.

[3] Liberati A, Altman DG, Tetzlaff J, et al. The PRISMA statement for reporting systematic reviews and meta-analyses of studies that evaluate health care interventions: explanation and elaboration. AnnIntern Med 2009;151:W65—94. https://doi.org/10.7326/0003-4819-151-4-200908180-00136.

Ethics in systematic reviews

18

Mahsa Ghajarzadeh[1] and Kiarash Aramesh[2]

[1]*Department of Neurology, Johns Hopkins University School of Medicine, Baltimore, MD, United States;* [2]*Department of Biology, Earth, and Environmental Sciences (BEES), The James F. Drane Bioethics Institute, PA, United States*

Introduction

Research ethics has been a growing field of study, especially in recent decades. Today, observing ethical considerations is an integral part of research activities from the beginning of designing the project through the conducting of the research to the final step, which is the publication of the findings. Today, researchers are required to pay strong attention to publication ethics. Therefore, various organizations are involved in publication ethics, such as:

(1) International Committee of Medical Journals Editors (ICMJE),
(2) World Association of Medical Editors (WAME),
(3) Committee on Publication Ethics (COPE).

The goal of all these organizations is to provide guidelines to avoid misconduct among authors, contributors, reviewers, and editors [1].

Systematic reviews are one of the major means of publishing research findings. However, their secondary nature may explain the unnecessity of an ethical assessment for most systematic reviews. Conducting systematic reviews primarily does not involve working with human subjects, so an ambiguity may arise about whether ethical consideration should be given to them. A systematic review is a review of multiple other studies that might have involved research on human or animal subjects. It is assumed that most studies included in systematic reviews have followed the relevant ethical guidelines (based on the study design), but in reality, this may not be accurate.

Weingarten et al. believed that ethical assessment of systematic reviews would show unethical primary studies with uncertain results [2]. This phenomenon may make the results of systematic reviews untrustworthy and unreliable.

The basic assumption for systematic reviews is that the primary studies included in the reviews respect fundamental ethical principles [3]. However, not all included studies followed complete ethical requirements, and ethical heterogeneity and quality assortment exist among them.

Systematic Review and Meta-Analysis. https://doi.org/10.1016/B978-0-443-13428-9.00018-5

The main purpose of including ethics in the checklist of systematic reviews is to pay increasing attention to the need for high ethical standards in medical research, especially in research that involves human subjects [4]. Ethical considerations for systematic reviews differ from those for original studies, and all included studies cannot be examined under the same microscope [2].

For systematic reviews, a comprehensive search (discussed in Chapter 5) is necessary to avoid missing published and nonpublished studies (publication bias). Such a comprehensive review is an ethical obligation; however, it may lead to the inclusion of unethical studies (that did not follow ethical basics).

Most researchers exclude studies with lesser quality assessment scores (based on each study type quality assessment score) from the final analysis of a systematic review, but the problem remains for conference abstracts that only report a summary of the method. There is no access to the full text to see if they followed the ethical guidelines or not. If these abstracts have large sample sizes, they would get higher weights in the meta-analysis, which would distort the final results.

Another major issue that raises ethical considerations for systematic reviews is the conflict of interest, especially for medicinal systematic reviews, which involve the link between researchers and drug companies. If systematic reviews are supported by industry, they may report conclusions that favor a sponsor's medication compared with systematic reviews without any relation to the industry [4,5].

To evaluate the ethical consideration of systematic reviews, in 2004, Weingarten et al. proposed a protocol to assess the ethics of systematic reviews, which was inspired by Foster's work focusing on the aim of the research, the moral duty of the researchers, rights of the participants of each study, and finally global ethical assessment of the research by an ethics committee [2,6].

Nowadays, The Measurement Tool to Assess Systematic Reviews (AMSTAR) is proposed to assess the methodological quality of systematic reviews [7]. Initially, the AMSTAR could only be applied to systematic reviews of clinical trials, but it could be applied to observational studies, too. It includes questions regarding conflict of interest, handling the impact of small study effects, risk of bias evaluation of included studies, and source of funding. However, most authors do not apply AMSTAR, and journals do not require its checklist as a mandatory supplement to systematic reviews, which may raise potential ethical uncertainty.

AMSTAR's limitation is that it does not include a report of the conflicts of interest of included trials and only asks about the sources of funding for included studies, which highlights the need for more consideration of conflict of interest in included studies.

Roseman et al. reviewed 29 systematic reviews, including 509 RCTs, and found that funding sources and conflicts of interest were rarely reported in systematic reviews [8].

Randomized control trials (RCTs)

Randomized Control Trials (RCTs) are the gold standard for evaluating the efficacy of an intervention or a medication and translating the data into clinical practice [9].

Awareness of ethical consideration of RCTs has increased over the years, and research ethics committees were set up after the declaration of Helsinki [2].

The Consolidated Standards of Reporting Trials (CONSORT) was developed in 1996 to improve the quality of reporting RCT results. It was updated in 2010 [10]. CONSORT includes items regarding the assessment of randomization, allocation, and blinding in RCTs to highlight the risk of bias [11].

For systematic reviews of clinical trials, some important points should be considered for each individual study:

1. It is important to check if the informed consent was obtained or not,
2. If the sample size was satisfactory,
3. If a conflict of interest and financial relationships are declared,
4. If the application of a placebo was acceptable or not,
5. If the comparators were the same or not,
6. If the study was approved by the local ethics committee or not,
7. If the clinical trial was registered before conduction.

If these items are not evaluable, systematic reviews will be away from recruitment. In 2011, Foster proposed a protocol to evaluate the ethics in systematic reviews considering:

1. The aims of the research,
2. The moral duty of the investigators,
3. Considering the rights of the subjects who are participating in the research,
4. Considering the global ethical assessment of the research by an ethics committee.

Unfortunately, these factors are not considered carefully in biomedical research [6].

Cochrane Risk of Bias Tool and JADAD are tools designed for the quality assessment of RCTs. They evaluate randomization, allocation, and blindness, but there is no option for obtaining informed consent, protocol registration, placebo administration, and comparison of the treatments. These limitations may result in the presence of bias in included RCTs. Also, Cochrane risk of bias assessment does not include objective observation assessment, which may cause follow-up bias [11]. So, all aspects of ethics are not evaluated using the Cochrane risk of bias tool or JADAD, leading to potential bias in systematic reviews, including these studies.

For systematic reviews of clinical trials, Weingarten et al. suggested the following guidelines (if these items were met) to evaluate before including RCTs:

1. A clear statement of funding,
2. Statement of conflict of interest,
3. Assessment of publication bias,
4. Appropriate comparators (justification of placebo administration),
5. Justification (large sample size to achieve adequate power, duplication of the results in the laboratory),
6. The risk of participation was low, and if appropriate, follow-up was done.

7. Was informed consent obtained?

8. Was there any guarantee to keep participants interested in the study?

9. Were data kept unauthorized and safe?

10. If the study was approved by a research ethics committee [2].

If these items are not evaluated in RCTs of systematic reviews, the pooled results will be biased.

In addition, the authors of systematic reviews need to observe general publication ethics principles such as avoiding redundancy and plagiarism [12].

Conclusions

Ethics may not be considered carefully in systematic reviews, especially in systematic reviews of interventions. It increases the responsibility of the systematic review conductors to pay attention to the ethical aspects of their work.

The authors of systematic reviews should pay attention to performing their literature review comprehensively, excluding any redundancies, avoiding plagiarism, and acknowledging all the contributors.

Editors of the journals may ask researchers to submit an AMSTAR form with their manuscript and report any ethical issues that they find in the included systematic review studies.

References

[1] Singhal S, Kalra BS. Publication ethics: role and responsibility of authors. Indian J Gastroenterol 2021;40:65–71.

[2] Weingarten MA, Paul M, Leibovici L. Assessing ethics of trials in systematic reviews. Br Med J 2004;328(7446):1013–4.

[3] Vergnes J-N, Marchal-Sixou C, Nabet C, Maret D, Hamel O. Ethics in systematic reviews. J Med Ethics 2010;36(12):771–4.

[4] Yank V, Rennie D, Bero LA. Financial ties and concordance between results and conclusions in meta-analyses: retrospective cohort study. Br Med J 2007;335(7631): 1202–5.

[5] Jørgensen AW, Hilden J, Gøtzsche PC. Cochrane reviews compared with industry supported meta-analyses and other meta-analyses of the same drugs: systematic review. Br Med J 2006;333(7572):782.

[6] Foster C. The ethics of medical research on humans. Cambridge University Press; 2001.

[7] Shea BJ, Grimshaw JM, Wells GA, Boers M, Andersson N, Hamel C, et al. Development of AMSTAR: a measurement tool to assess the methodological quality of systematic reviews. BMC Med Res Methodol 2007;7:1–7.

[8] Roseman M, Milette K, Bero LA, Coyne JC, Lexchin J, Turner EH, et al. Reporting of conflicts of interest in meta-analyses of trials of pharmacological treatments. JAMA 2011;305(10):1008–17.

[9] Cuschieri S. The CONSORT statement. Saudi J Anaesth 2019;13(Suppl. 1):S27.

[10] Eldridge SM, Chan CL, Campbell MJ, Bond CM, Hopewell S, Thabane L, et al. CON-SORT 2010 statement: extension to randomised pilot and feasibility trials. Br Med J 2016;355.

[11] Paneque RJ, Bachelet VC. Los ensayos clínicos y su publicación-las guías CONSORT en primer plano Clinical trials and study reporting-CONSORT guidelines at the forefront.

[12] Wager E, Wiffen PJ. Ethical issues in preparing and publishing systematic reviews. J Evid Base Med 2011;(4):130−4.

Index

Printed in the United States
by Baker & Taylor Publisher Services